Unyielding Hope:
The Life and Times of Koitaleel Somoei

KIPCHOGE araap CHOMU
and
GILES HUMPHRY

First published in 2012 by
Phoenix Publishers Ltd.
Mellow Heights, Ngara Road,
P.O Box 303474-00100,
Nairobi.

© Text: Kipchoge araap Chomu and Giles Humphry, 2012
© Illustrations: Phoenix Publishers Ltd. 2012

ISBN 9966 47 846 9

All effort has been put in getting permission for all copyrighted text quoted in this book. However, should any have been inadvertently left out, the publisher would be glad to make the necessary arrangements at the earliest convenience.

Contents

Dedication v

Acknowledgments vi

Why we write vii

Introduction ix

Chapter 1: Once upon a time … 1

Chapter 2: The rising of the sun 15

Chapter 3: Seeds of the struggle 27

Chapter 4: Confounding the British Empire 36

Chapter 5: A messenger from Hell 59

Chapter 6: The sun goes down 70

Chapter 7: Grand finale 87

Dedication

In memory of Martin James Parry, without whose vision, dedication and unfailing generosity this book would never have been born.

1961-2012

No kinder soul.

No truer friend.

Acknowledgments

This book is the work of many hands. Cheruiyot Araap Koskei has earned first place in the roll of honour by his invaluable assistance at every stage of the project. Gratitude is likewise due to the Reverend Sylas Tochim for commitment, enthusiasm and ability to make things happen. Thereafter, Dr Kipkoeech Sambu is deserving of honour for his extraordinarily generous help in so many areas, above and beyond the call of duty, including helping us to hunt down errors in the early draft. Any mistakes that remain are our own. Former Acting Ambassador Jacob Chumba has been no less liberal with his time and the fruits of his research and deserves enduring gratitude for his help in producing an accurate biography. Brian Garfield, author of "The Meinertzhagen Mystery" and other fine works showed great kindness in helping us with our own researches, which followed in his footsteps.

As for our literary sources, *The Meinertzhagen Mystery* was irreplaceable as also was A.T. Matson's authoritative work, *Nandi Resistance to British Rule*. Meanwhile, Bill Rutto's prologue to the second volume of Matson's work, provides the reader with the best brief introduction to the conflict between the Nandi and the British. Other sources are listed in the bibliography.

Praise is due to John Mwazemba, CEO of Phoenix publishers, for his commitment to producing a great book at short notice. Sentences beginning with "and" and "but" are not due to any oversight on the part of the proofreaders at Phoenix but to the authorial insistence that no purported rule can outweigh the authority of the compilers of the King James Bible, which often starts sentences thus. The decision to follow the phonetic system of Kalenjin spelling (causing our spelling to deviate sometimes from other sources), was also our own. Thanks are owed also to Tracy Veck for her help and advice.

Why we write

Koitaleel Somoei, the supreme leader of the Nandi people of Kenya spearheaded the resistance to the British invasion of Kenya at the end of the nineteenth century. Under his leadership, the Nandi held fast to their freedom for more than a decade in the face of a series of British campaigns and police actions. Given that Koitaleel commanded perhaps 3,000 warriors, the achievement of the Nandi surely earns them a place in the pantheon of freedom's heroes alongside those ancient Spartans who frustrated the Persian invasion of Greece. It is true that King Leonidas of Sparta had just 300 men to Koitaleel's 3,000 and that the legendary horde of the Persian King Xerxes was vastly greater than any force that the British brought against the Nandi. Yet it is also true that, whereas the Nandi, like both the Spartans and Persians, fought with spears and bows, the British Empire exceeded the Persian in both extent and development and possessed over it the inestimable advantage of the Maxim gun, which would have made mincemeat of Leonidas' shield wall in minutes. Then too, the Nandi held out for over ten years compared with the six days that the Spartans held up the Persians. This work tells the remarkable story of the man who led this freedom struggle and who was murdered by the British during the course of a peace conference.

The joint authorship of this book, with one Kenyan and one British author and our dependence on both British and Kenyan sources is reflective of our intention to write something more than another anti-colonial history. It is not that we wish to be neutral between colonialism and its victims. It is rather that we believe that while historians may judge, their primary duty is to help the reader understand and there is much in this account that may tax the reader's understanding. How was it possible that within the lifespan of a few still living, deeds that would today be hidden from the light of day were honoured as patriotic acts, to the extent that the murderer of Koitaleel was recommended for a Victoria Cross for his crime? How were so small a people as the Nandi able to withstand so great an Empire as the British for so long? Why did the British, despite possessing overwhelming technical superiority over the Nandi, feel it necessary to resort to treachery in order to crush them?

Between the modern Kenyan or British reader and their ancestors at the turn of the Nineteenth and Twentieth centuries lies a gulf that can be crossed only by a leap of imagination. The British have surrendered their Empire, the Nandi likewise have forsworn the right to subjugate others and have accepted their place in the family of peoples that is the nation of Kenya. At the time of our story, however, both British and Nandi believed themselves to be entitled to dominate others and each was prepared to use any necessary means to secure what they saw as their birthright. We believe that to understand our ancestors is to understand ourselves. If, therefore, we can assist the reader in understanding how those so near to us in time could yet behave so differently, we will consider our labours well rewarded.

Kipchoge araap Chomu and Giles Humphry

Introduction

The beginning of the modern era is most usually placed in 1492, the year when Columbus "discovered" America. At that time, the Kenyan city of Mombasa was a great and thriving port, a centre of dealing in spices, ivory and gold, with trade links to China and India.

Had a Mombasan of this era made his way to London, it is likely that he would have regarded it as a rather squalid little town. At this time, Europe had hardly begun the process of "civilisation", either in the objective and original sense of urbanisation or the subjective senses of cultural refinement and decent behaviour. One of the first things a Kenyan traveller might have noticed would have been the Londoners' offensive smell, though this would have gone unremarked by those from elsewhere in Europe, which has justly been described as "the continent that did not wash for a thousand years".

The next century saw some progress in habits of cleanliness to the extent that it would be commented with wonder of the first queen Elizabeth that she bathed once a month "whether she needed it or not", though the quote has survived in various forms and other versions attribute quarterly, biannual or yearly bathing to this paragon of hygiene. By the nineteenth century, we have the first example of a great Briton – the Duke of Wellington – who bathed daily, a habit he appears to have picked up in India. However, his adoption of this foreign custom was regarded as a disturbing eccentricity excusable only against the background of the duke's great services to his country. At any rate, at the dawn of the modern era, Europeans had yet to take the first step on the long march to cleanliness and our Kenyan could have counted himself lucky to find a Londoner who bathed more than once a year.

Had he wished for entertainment, our Mombasan traveller might have chosen to attend a hanging, enlivened if he was lucky by the pulling out of the victim's entrails and the dismemberment of his body. Alternatively, he might have amused himself by throwing stones or rotten eggs at an offender in the stocks. Had he hoped to find more refined pleasures though, he would very likely have been disappointed.

By contrast, a Kenyan travelling to other parts of the world would have had a much more enlightening experience. In China, he could have witnessed the world's most exquisitely-refined culture, though he might have noticed that it was as refined in its cruelties as its pleasures. In India, too, he would have found an ancient, prosperous and developed civilisation. Meanwhile, had he somehow made his way to the Americas, he could have witnessed what was probably the greatest city ever to grace this world– Tenochtitlan, a marvellous place of canals and palaces, fragrant gardens and soaring pyramids, the steps of which, however, were stained with the blood of human sacrifice. Had he managed to discover Australia, he could even have encountered an essentially non-violent people that saw no point in technical progress when they had everything they could possibly need from the natural bounty of that great continent.

During the "modern era" initiated by Columbus, European civilisation would flourish as never before. At the same time, the other civilisations and cultures just described would be crushed underfoot by the spread of European colonialism. Tenochtitlan would be systematically dismantled by the Spanish, The Summer Palace of Peking burnt to the ground, India would be subjugated and looted and the Aboriginal people of Australia would be rudely awakened from their dreaming to be hunted like animals. Slavery, which had virtually died out in Europe, would be revived on an industrial scale as millions were transported from Africa to the Americas to replace the labour of the people that the Europeans had so carelessly wiped out.

To justify these atrocities, "colour prejudice" was invented. A hierarchy of races was constructed with the lightest skinned at the top and the darkest at the bottom. This form of racism had been almost unknown in pre-modern Europe. The Romans might have massacred or enslaved entire peoples but they did not justify this on the grounds that their victims had a different skin colour. Indeed, it was white peoples such as the Britons and Germans who served for the Romans as the paradigm of barbarism. Cicero warned his fellow Romans not to buy British slaves as their stupidity made them unteachable. In Mediaeval Europe, the great divide was between Christians and Moslems; skin colour was a matter of irrelevance, at least on the Christian side. A 10th century Moslem scholar did observe that Europeans grew more pale the farther North they were and that the "farther they are to the North the more stupid, gross and brutish they are". Yet as Thomas Sowell notes, although this would be classified as racism today, in the historical context, it was simply an accurate observation of European backwardness.

In the modern era, by contrast, the mistreatment of non-Europeans came to be substantially justified on the basis of the moral and cultural superiority of white people. The obvious political utility of this doctrine caused it to spread rapidly despite its novelty and inherent absurdity. That the adoption of colour prejudice was in the first instance opportunistic may be illustrated by the fact that the earliest American colonists were quite happy to make use of "slaves" of all colours, Native American and white as well as black. So, for example, children were seized from the streets of Britain's cities and transported into "slavery" in the American colonies. However, Native Americans knew the land and were able to live off it if they escaped. Escaped white "slaves" found it easy to blend into the background and pass themselves off as free. Black "slaves", by contrast, were disorientated by the long journey from Africa, did not know the land and could not pass themselves off as free colonists.

At this point, "slavery" actually referred to bonded labour, a form of forced labour that was, in theory, time-limited and non-hereditary. The usefulness of black bonded labourers led to the reintroduction of legally-recognised hereditary chattel slavery for black people, a development excused by the notion of non-white inferiority that was already gaining ground as a general justification for the suppression of non-Europeans.

Nevertheless, the historically novel notion that black people were uniquely suited to the condition of slavery was never universally accepted. In North Africa, where hereditary chattel slavery had never died out, the Arabs continued to enslave white, brown and black without discrimination. Thus, there were English slaves in North Africa right up until the final suppression of the slave trade. Even in Europe, the invention of colour prejudice did not go unchallenged. The Catholic Church condemned the enslavement and mistreatment of non-Europeans. The proclamation of human equality by American and French revolutionaries was taken by the more consistent among them to include black people and this ideal gave impetus to the campaign for the abolition of slavery.

This campaign finally succeeded in converting the British Empire, leading to the suppression of the slave trade by the Royal navy during the Empire's second finest hour. It would, nevertheless, be a mistake to see the abolition of slavery as a turning point in the struggle against racism. While some abolitionists did indeed preach racial equality, many others did not. Thus, for example, Abraham Lincoln in 1858, said, "I am not, nor ever have been, in favour of bringing about in any way the social and political equality of the white and black races…I am not, nor ever have been, in favour of making voters or jurors of negroes, nor of qualifying them to hold office, nor to intermarry with white people."

In fact, by the end of the nineteenth century, colour prejudice was probably more securely established than it had been at the start and imperialism was at the peak of its brutality. In British India, millions died in famines at a time when India had a surplus of rice, which was being exported to Britain. Private efforts to relieve famine victims were prohibited. Relief camps set up by the Raj had a monthly death rate of 94% as Indians were worked to death and fed less than the inhabitants of Buchenwald. When the Indians searched for food on "Crown land" (their traditional common lands), they were mutilated and branded. Other European powers outdid the British in cruelty. In the Belgian Congo, as many as 10 million Africans may have perished at Belgian hands, and millions more were maimed. Translated into modern money, the profit extracted by the Belgian King from his crimes was around 500 million Euros, or fifty Euros for each life destroyed – considerably less than would be demanded by a common hitman. This, putting no price on the piles of children's limbs. The brual acts in the Congo were just one facet of the expansion of European colonialism into the interior of Africa, which included the subjugation of Kenya.

Thus, a descendant of our original Kenyan mariner, travelling to London for the Diamond Jubilee of Queen Victoria in 1897, would have had a very different experience from his ancestor at the start of the modern era. He would have found a vast and thriving metropolis serving as the nerve centre of the greatest empire the world had ever seen. He would have discovered that, at least amongst the middle and upper classes, cleanliness was next to godliness and that cultural refinement was a prerequisite of social acceptability. He might have been gratified to discover that when the beaten Zulu King, Cetewayo, had come to London a few years earlier, the common people, though they had been incited by the press to view him as a beast, had nonetheless chosen to honour him as a man. Imitating the magnanimity of the Emperor Claudius to their ancestor Caractacus, they had cheered themselves hoarse whenever Cetewayo had shown himself abroad. He should also have been pleased that Queen Victoria, notorious for her lack of colour prejudice, had received the African monarch most warmly. Then too, had he previously visited the United States with its "Jim Crow" laws, he would have been favourably impressed by the fact that British law did not formally segregate different races. Yet had he stayed long enough, he would have learnt that an informal code can bear down with no less force than whips and chains and that amongst the classes intervening between Queen and commons, even an African king would have been viewed as standing considerably lower than an Indian prince, let alone an English gentleman, and would have been received by many in society only as a novelty akin to a talking ape. Moreover, while a Kenyan might have expected a gracious reception from Queen Victoria had he been introduced, his pleasure would surely have been tempered by the fact that he would have been required to honour her as the rightful ruler of his own country.

Any Kenyan would have been well aware that this claim to sovereignty was still hotly contested by many of his own compatriots. For, from 1895 until 1905, the best laid plans of British colonial administrators would be repeatedly frustrated by a remarkable campaign of guerrilla resistance. The focus of this anti-colonial struggle was the territory of the Nandi community and its leader, the Kenyan Spartacus, was Koitaleel Somoei araap Kimnyolei.

Chapter 1

Once upon a time ...

The Nandi belong to a family of peoples claiming common ancestry, which today are known as the Kalenjin. According to Nandi oral history, the ancestors of the Kalenjin peoples were warriors in Pharaonic Egypt and stood close to the throne. Support for this thesis is supplied both from similarities between the Kalenjin language and that of ancient Egypt and from consideration of the Kalenjin's ancestral religion. This is essentially monotheistic, that is, based on the belief in one all-powerful God. This religion was based on worship of a supreme deity ruling over a world of spirits. The name of God is Assiis who is the source of all things. The symbol of Assiis is the sun, though the sun is not itself God.

Scholars of Anciet Egypt will immediately recognise that this faith echoes that of the 18th dynasty Pharaoh, Akhenaton. Akhenaton preached a single supreme God in place of Egypt's traditional polytheism – belief in many gods. He called his God "the Aton" and "the mother and father of mankind". The symbol of the Aton was the sun disc. In Kalenjin, Aton means spirit. This novel religion was abandoned by Akhenaton's son and successor – the boy king and priestly puppet, Tutankhamun, who restored Egypt's ancient pantheon of gods and goddesses.

The same Tutankhamun was at the centre of a recent controversy that may shed some light on our story. In 2005, the National Geographic produced a reconstruction of the Pharaoh's face based on a CT scan of his skull. The resulting picture was of an olive-skinned gentleman with Euro-Asiatic features. Afrocentrists in the United States were outraged, accusing National Geographic of participating in a racist conspiracy to hide the fact that Tutankhamun had been black. Zahi Hawass, head of Egypt's Supreme Council of Antiquities, retorted, "Tutankhamun was not black and the portrayal of ancient Egyptian civilisation as black has no element of truth in it."

It was Hawass who led a team of scientists who performed DNA tests on the 18th dynasty mummies to establish the relationships between them. A Swiss DNA testing company claimed to have deduced, from watching the tests being performed on the Discovery Channel, that Tutankhamun had a white ancestor in the direct male line. Hawass' team denied that this conclusion could be drawn from the publicly available evidence, but refused to publish their full results and conclusions. If the Swiss company is correct, it suggests the unlikely conclusion that Hawass chose to suppress evidence that supported his own case. Meanwhile, another company, "DNA Tribes", has concluded that the closest modern relatives of the 18th dynasty would be populations in southern Africa and the Great Lakes region (which includes Kenya).

Here, we must weigh certain other evidence tending to support the Afrocentrist case. Thus, though National Geographic gave Tutankhamun a "white" nose based on the CT scan of his nasal cavity, one gets a different picture if one looks at his actual mummified nose.

That looks much broader and flatter, like the noses on his statues and those of his grandfather Amenhotep III. The mummy also displays fleshy prominent lips like his statues and those of both his father and grandfather. Meanwhile, his skin colour is depicted in a variety of tones from jet black, through a rich red brown, to beige. This is testimony to the fact that skin tone was a matter of irrelevance to the Egyptians. It is, therefore, conceivable in principle that he was white, the one colour he was never portrayed. However, as the Pharaoh would have been sheltered from the oppressive heat, if he was white he could never have had even the lightest of the skin shades in which he ordered himself to be depicted.

We might also consider the allegedly peculiar skull shape of the 18th dynasty Pharaohs, distinguished by an "elongated" cranium. A team of scientists who scanned Tutankhamun's skull without being told whose it was identified the cranium as probably African. As Dr Kipkoeech araap Sambu has pointed out, the skull shape is typical of certain African peoples, notably the Kalenjin. In other words, if Tutankhamun had "white genes", they seem to have produced a king with a "black" skull, nose and lips and who was always portrayed as non-white. To add to the confusion, his grandmother – Queen Tiye – is also portrayed with black skin and features, yet she is believed to have possessed Semitic ancestry and reddish hair. Meanwhile, the whole family is portrayed with "Asian eyes" though this may simply have been due to the Egyptian habit of painting their eyes to look almond-shaped.

Perhaps the safest bolt hole in this racial controversy would be to view the 18th dynasty as mixed race, a bland description, which potentially encompasses a great number of Egypt's Pharaohs. Our own inclination is to side with the majority of Egyptologists who feel that the whole attempt to pigeonhole ancient Egyptians into modern racial categories that would have been incomprehensible to them is misplaced.

Nevertheless, we do not believe it is meaningless to ask about the kinship ties of the 18th dynasty Pharaohs. For example, if these rulers were kin to the ancestors of the Kalenjin, then it could explain why this people group remained loyal to the revelation of Akhenaton, long after it had been forgotten by other Egyptians. Notwithstanding Tutankhamun's apostasy, the religion of the Aton was the unique contribution of the 18th dynasty to Egypt's history. If their genius was kept alive after the dynasty's demise, it would not be surprising to find that it was their kin group that kept the flame burning. We do not say that it must have been so, only that it may have been and that there must have been some reason why the Kalenjin's forefathers remained faithful to Akhenaton's legacy. It may be relevant here that the red haired Ramses II, the most famous Pharaoh of the 19th dynasty, recycled some of the statues of Tutankhamun's grandfather, Amenhotep III, by ordering their lips to be made thinner so as to look more like himself. The Egyptians would not have thought of this as "whitening" but, applying modern categories to the Ancient World, that is how we would probably describe Ramses' action. To put it another way, while it is plausible to suggest a close relationship between the 18th dynasty Pharaohs and the ancestors of the Nilotic peoples (the larger people group which includes the Kalenjin), the same cannot be said with respect to the 19th dynasty. And if the proto-Nilotic people group was related to the former dynasty but not the latter it would have cemented their loyalty to the legacy of Akhenaton.

At first, such faithfulness would not have been too difficult. Tutankhamun is unlikely to have approved the persecution of his father's followers. Some think that by the end of his brief reign, he was beginning to shake off the grip of his priestly councillors and rehabilitate his father's revelation. Perhaps he envisaged some sort of fusion between Akhenaton's monotheism and Egypt's traditional polytheism. It may have been in such a spirit that the worshippers of the Aton first began to worship the one God under the guise of Isis, the queen of Egypt's gods whose name has been preserved as Assiis in Kalenjin. Alternatively, this change may have been adopted as an attempt to ward off persecution under Tutankhamun's successors, who sought to erase all record of Akhenaton and his religion. Either way, at some point, the ancestors of the Kalenjin found the persecution too hot to handle. They decided to leave Egypt to find a land of their own.

Those who place no weight on oral history may say that the evidence we have cited for these claims is thin; the alleged preservation of the religion and name of Aton, certain similarities between the Kalenjin and Egyptian languages and a coincidence between the skull shapes of the 18th dynasty Pharaohs and those of the modern day Kalenjin. Against such scepticism we would argue that important truths may be passed down by word of mouth and that our oral history slots neatly into what we know of 18th and 19th dynasty Egypt. Meanwhile, we would refer readers interested in a more thorough examination of the evidence to Dr Kipkoeech Sambu's forthcoming book, *The Military Clan of Pharaoh*.

Others have argued that "Kalenjin" remained in Egypt long after the 19th dynasty, and this may well be so. Nevertheless, the subsequent disappearance from the Egyptian record of all trace of the religion of Aton suggests a 19th dynasty time frame for the original exodus of the worshippers of Aton/Assiis. Any who remained in Egypt would have had to keep their faith secret. Even so, it is possible that some managed to do so and that the ancestors of different Nilotic groups may have left Egypt at different times. This might explain why the name for God differs from one Nilotic group to another, despite a common commitment to monotheism.

The Egyptian origin stories of the Nilotic peoples have been mocked by some who ask why these communities did not recreate anything like the civilisation of Egypt in their new lands. The sceptics suggest Nubia (roughly modern Sudan) as an alternative point of origin for the Nilotes. The problem for the sceptics is that Nubia was also a highly developed civilisation, which built great pyramids and temples. Thus, the question they pose still needs to be answered if one proposes a Nubian origin for the Nilotic peoples. Nor is the problem solved by moving the motherland to Ethiopia, also a sophisticated culture. These African civilisational triumphs are often obscured by the debate over who owns Egypt, but they were real, nonetheless.

The question posed by the sceptics is in any case easy to answer. In order to support a large population in dry lands, one needs a high level of technical development including irrigation and a centralised state. It was on such a foundation that the civilisations of Egypt and Nubia rested. By contrast, the territories to which the Kalenjin and others moved were lands of milk and honey. If one can obtain everything one needs with a minimum of effort, the necessity for a high level of technical development disappears.

The legends do not tell us the full history of the Kalenjin's wanderings. What they do say is that prior to their emigration to the territories they now occupy, the Kalenjin were living in such a land of milk and honey. Quite possibly, the stories combine several rich areas that the ancestors occupied into a single legend. At any rate, the territory occupied prior to the final migration appears to have lain to the north of the Great Rift Valley near Kenya's freshwater Lake Baringo. It was a green and fertile place, home to numerous species of animals, birds, fish and plants. In those days, the people were upright, children honoured their elders, women their men and men their God.

It was to this God, to Assiis, that the Kalenjin would turn when their idyll in the land was rudely interrupted. By the 17th century AD, a change in climate had caused a drying up of the rivers. Formerly green lands became parched and the hordes of game and flocks of birds departed. The people's flesh fell off and mothers had no milk to suckle their children. Many feared not just for their own lives but for the very existence of their nation. With one voice, the Kalenjin beseeched Assiis to send them a sign. At the point when all seemed lost and the people doomed, a miracle occurred. One night, bats were seen flying in from the South with grass in their mouths. This showed that there was fertile land in the direction from which they came. Thus, this time of trial became known as "the famine of the bats".

As Ian Orchardson described in *The Kipsigis*, three parties of eight warriors each were sent to spy out the new Promised Land, one party from each of the war divisions into which the community was then divided. On their return, the elders asked each party what omens they had encountered. One party had met only three good omens on the outward journey and none on the return. The division represented by this group decided to stay near where they then lived. They became the Tugen, the Keiyo and the Marakwet. Another party had met five good omens on the outward journey but none on the way back. Their group determined to trek to the lands that had been discovered and in the process became the Kipsigis. The final party had met four omens on the outward journey and one on their way back. Four being a sacred number to the Kalenjin, it was concluded that this group had found the richest cattle country. This fortunate division became the people who would be known as the Nandi.

The migration to the new lands was a gradual process. Those who were least weakened by famine were sent ahead first to establish themselves before returning for the others. The first area to be settled in was named after one Kakipooch. The land of the community that became known as the Nandi is to be found in the South West corner of a hilly area, which merges into the Uasin Nkishu plateau to the East and which is bounded by high slopes and cliffs to the West and the South. The altitude – thousands of feet above sea level

– moderates the African heat and the climate is kind and healthy, avoiding uncomfortable extremes. The land is generously watered by three rivers and rainfall is plentiful between March and September. Both wooded areas and grazing lands abound, oat grass being the most common kind.

The smallest political unit of the Nandi was the neighbourhood or *koret*. Each of these was self-governing with regard to its internal affairs with all married men sharing in decision making. Disputes between neighbourhoods were handed over to the council of the *Pororiet,* a larger division that was both a territorial and a military unit and whose name implies the equality of its members. A *Pororiet* might perhaps be compared to a republic in time of peace and to a militia regiment in wartime. The Nandi community as a whole might thus be seen either as a confederation of republics or as an alliance of militias, depending on whether one views them at peace or at war. These "regiments" were not clans, the various extended Nandi families that deserve this name were scattered across different *pororyoosiek* (plural of Pororiet). Therefore, the Nandi's political system helped to bind different clans together in both war and peace and to regulate their rivalries.

As a result of the leapfrog manner in which Nandi was settled, separated territories might be part of a single *Pororiet* area. This was a lucky accident as it ensured that clan rivalries were not replaced by territorial splits since such divisions would have left the outposts of some regiments cut off from their home territories. As a result, disputes between different regiments were settled not by war but with mock battles using whips and sticks. The Nandi's regimental system gave them a definite advantage when facing other peoples divided by clan rivalries and territorial disputes. For a community with just a few thousand active warriors, it was a much needed head start over more numerous enemies. The number of regiments is sometimes given as 15 or 16. This total counts some subdivisions of the original *pororyoosiek* as regimental areas in their own right. In fact, there were just twelve original regiments of the Nandi: the Kakipooch, the Kapchepkendi, the Kamelilo, the Kaptalam, the Kaptumoiis, the Kapianga, the Koilegei, the Kikimno, the Kapsiondoi, the Kapsile, the Kapwareng and the Tiping'ot.

Like the other Kalenjin, the Nandi were by tradition cattle herders and warriors. They lived on terms of great intimacy with their cattle, which were regarded almost as family members. Cattle were not only the measure of a man's wealth, the source of blood and milk to drink and meat to eat, but also the focus of tribal existence. Sheep and goats were kept and the Nandi did not disdain to hunt, fish or raise crops but none mistook these activities for the real business of life. They held it to be self evident that this lay in the tending and acquisition of cattle. At the times of which we write, "acquisition" meant primarily cattle raiding – skill in raiding and the display of martial valour were regarded as the true tests of manhood. Raids were generally conducted by one or two regiments and regarded in the light of a sport.

The leadership of the community was provided by the Oorgooik, holy men whose blessing was sought before any raid was undertaken. The position of the Oorgooik paralleled that of the Maasai "Laibons", seers who discerned the will of Heaven and the prospects of victory by a combination of shrewd use of spies and divination.

There was repeated conflict between the Nandi and the Maasai, particularly the neighbouring Uasin Nkishu Maasai. This struggle was resolved in favour of the Nandi after their victory at *Mogobich* near present day *Ollessos* when the Maasai were driven away from Nandi lands. *Mooki,* a widow of the Maasai, pregnant by her late husband, was prevented by her condition from joining the flight of her people. She hid herself in a cave at *Keben* and gave birth to twins, Kopogoi and

Barsapotwo. The family was adopted by two lions, which protected them and brought them food.

When the boys had grown, they came out of the cave to play and were seen by some Nandi herdsmen. The herdsmen wanted to capture the boys but the boys would run into the cave where the lions would protect them. The Nandi met and deliberated on ways to persuade the family to leave the protection of the lions and the lions to let the family go. The decision was made to approach the elders of the Talai clan. Each clan of the Nandi has one or more animal totems. Thus, the Kipyegen have the baboon and the house mouse, the Kipkenda identify with the bee and the frog, the Kipkoitim have the elephant, the chameleon and the rabbit. The symbol of the Talai clan is the lion, hence the decision to seek their help. The Talai went and persuaded the family to join them and the lions to release Mooki and her sons to their care. Thus, Mooki, Kopogoi and Barsapotwo were adopted into the Talai clan and settled in south Aldai. The boys grew to be responsible and wise young men, though it was Kopogoi who took the lead since Barsapotwo had a tendency to being disant and unapproachable.

Then a drought came that dried up most of the rivers and water basins in Aldai, forcing the herdsmen to travel further and further in search of water. This led to an opportunity for Kopogoi to manifest his miraculous powers. Kopogoi could strike the ground causing a stream of clear water to flow so that his herd could quench their thirst. After watering the entire herd, he would strike the ground again and the stream would dry up.

These uncommon incidents were reported to the senior members of the community who at once realised that a seer was amongst them. The elders grilled Mooki, who confessed that her late husband had been a Maasai Laibon. Kopogoi was placed under a wise man who prepared him for the role of chief Oorgoiyoot, an office that had fallen vacant and which was revived especially for him. When he had completed his apprenticeship, he was enthroned as the first Nandi chief Oorgoiyoot of a new dynasty. The role of the Oorgoiyoot was to divine the will of Heaven and to foretell the future by such means as inspecting entrails, studying the natural world, interpreting dreams and casting lots. He was expected to prophesy and to bless and curse in the name of Assiis, to give advice, to serve as a focus of tribal unity and to preside over religious ceremonies. His person was sacred, no weapons could be brought into his presence, nor could he be addressed without invitation. No military action could be launched without his approval. As for succession, the Oorgoiyoot chose his heir from amongst his sons in accordance with the omens.

The authority of the Oorgoiyoot was symbolised by three batons. The forked baton represented the spiritual authority of the Oorgoiyoot to bless and to curse. The long-shafted "Siariit" staff represented his administrative role. The "Runguut" baton was used to give guidance to warriors before raids and other military expeditions.

Under the leadership of Kopogoi, an attempt by the Maasai to regroup and reclaim the land they had lost was decisively defeated and the supremacy of the Nandi over their neighbours was firmly established. Thus, Nandi dominance over the Maasai and other communities was entrenched by the adoption of a Maasai family and the imitation of the Maasai leadership structure. The Nandi were neither too proud to copy a good idea nor yet so insular as to reject immigrants willing to assimilate and to join the ranks of the people. However, one tradition holds that the Maasai Laibons who assimilated into the Nandi were descended from Nandi Oorgooik who had formerly assimilated into the Maasai.

From Kopogoi and Barsapotwo are descended the five families of the Talai Oorgooik; Kaapturugat, Kaapsogoon, Kaapmararsoi, Kaapsaneet and

Kaapchesang. After Kopogoi's death, the mantle of spiritual leadership passed to his son Turugat and later to Kimnyolei son of Turugat, who reigned after 1880. Kimnyolei was thus the third Nandi chief Oorgoiyoot and not the fourth as some have stated, on the erroneous assumption that the office of Oorgoiyoot was at some point shared, either by Kopogoi and Barsapotwo or by Turugat and his brother Mararsoi. Koitaleel, meanwhile, was the fourth chief Oorgoiyoot of his dynasty, not the fifth as is sometimes claimed.

Kimnyolei attained a pre-eminence that exceeded even that of his father and grandfather and the earlier years of his reign are remembered as a time of victory and prosperity. The raids that he blessed returned with plenty of cattle and usually unscathed. The Nandi extended their lands, peace and harmony prevailed between different clans and regiments and famine became a distant memory. Their neighbours did not dare to attack the regional superpower and the only conflicts were those initiated by the Nandi. The Oorgoiyoot's devotion to Assiis set an example to all, the people remembered Assiis in all their doings, and neither did they forget to honour the ancestors. When Kimnyolei's rulings were disobeyed, the offenders came to grief. Thus, on one occasion, he gave a blessing to a raiding party but advised them that, on the way back, they should not eat of any dead animal that they encountered. The raid was successful and the warriors returned in high spirits. But Kimnyolei saw into their hearts and solemnly charged them to answer truthfully whether they had faithfully observed his ruling. The warriors admitted that they had encountered a dead buffalo on the road home and that they had skinned and eaten it, thinking it a crime to let a free feast go to waste. The Oorgoiyoot was angered and ordered them to isolate themselves from the people. It was a wise precaution, it transpired the buffalo had died of anthrax and that the meat had infected those who had eaten of it.

Kimnyolei improved the system of government, reintroducing the cabinet system used by former dynasties and *maotik*, who carried messages between the Oorgoiyoot and the regiments. He always made sure that he consulted as widely as possible. As befitted a great man, Kimnyolei had three wives distinguished by their grace and beauty. There was Cheepo Kokwarei who bore no children, Cheepo Teitamuk who gave her husband three sons and Tapratoor Cheepo Kaapleu, the mother of Koitaleel.

Now the birth of Koitaleel was as follows. In 1860, many years before Kimnyolei's enthronement, when he was still known only as the son of Turugat, his wife Tapratoor was delivered of a child. This occurred at the time of Assiis, the moment when the first rays of the dawn begin to put the darkness of night time to flight. As the women that attended the lying in of Tapratoor raised their voices in the customary ululation to celebrate the infant's birth, their souls were filled with awe. For, from the face of the newborn that Tapratoor held up for their inspection, there blazed the red eyes that signified the gift of second sight. A prophet had been born.

Yet Kimnyolei could not join the rejoicing over his son's birth. Tapratoor had discovered she was pregnant while staying with her mother and the probable moment of conception coincided with that of her departure from her husband's home. Before parting, the couple had made love, but Kimnyolei could not shake off the suspicion that Tapratoor might have taken a lover while under her mother's roof and thus was tormented by the fear that another man might be the father of her child. Therefore, he decided to appeal to the judgement of Heaven and decreed that the boy be placed in the bull pen. "If the boy is the fruit of my loins," he reasoned, "Assiis will move the bulls to pity and spare his life. If he is trampled underfoot, then I will know he was no child of mine."

So the babe was placed in the centre of the pen and all watched carefully to see how he would fare, Kimnyolei hoping for the child's survival no less than his wife. Soon, their anxiety turned to marvel. The bulls not only took care not to trample the infant, they actually jumped over him when crossing the pen. When the ordeal was over and it was clear to all that the boy was sheltered by the hand of God, Kimnyolei rushed into the bull pen and took up his son, holding him high for all to see. "This is my son" he declared, "and he shall be a rock to crush his enemies and a bull to gore them". Thus, he was named Koitaleel, the rock and Somoei, after a bull in his father's herd.

Chapter 2

The rising of the sun

The red eyes of Koitaleel distinguished him from other children, so also did the fact that his left arm was somewhat shorter than his right. In a less favoured child, such a peculiarity might have been regarded as a bad omen. However, a child of royal blood, enjoying so many signs of Assiis' favour, would not be seen as possessing a foreshortened left arm. Rather, he would be seen as the owner of an exceptionally strong right arm, suited to a warrior destined to do battle on behalf of his people. He was further distinguished by his skin tone, which was of that coal-black shade that Africans sometimes refer to as "blue" and thus, dark even by the standards of the Nandi. His face was broad with a large forehead and his teeth appeared particularly white against his dark gums. Two of these teeth were later removed to create a *Kapyotit* or tooth gap, a feature admired by the Nandi.

Koitaleel was not raised by his birth mother Tapratoor but by another of his father's wives, Cheepo Kokwarei, Kimnyolei's favourite, who was childless. Koitaleel himself was shown no favouritism by his father and at mealtimes, he was always served last. Perhaps because of this, he would devour his food quickly, earning himself the nickname of *Kimanyei* – he who swallows without chewing. It was the only respect in which Koitaleel ever showed any lack of self control. As he got older, he was increasingly marked by his calmness of manner and his habit of thinking hard and consulting with others before taking any decision of his importance. When asked for advice, he always took his time to reply and was a good listener who genuinely cared about the problems of others. He was distinguished also by his courage, without ever falling into recklessness or disrespect to his elders.

As a man, he grew to no great height but had a powerful presence. Though not vain, he took some care of his appearance, sporting a small beard and earrings – copper loops adorned with knobs in his ear lobes, little rods with beads on each end through the upper ear. His clothes were made from the skins of blue or grey monkeys and, on his head, he wore an upwards-pointing hat made from a Colobus monkey. He carried an ivory pot with a chain handle to store tobacco, his only vice. He drank but rarely, on special occasions and, despite his childhood nickname, he was no glutton, dining mainly on the porridge gruel known as *Kimnyeet* made from millet and sorghum flour.

Even before reaching manhood, Koitaleel was followed by others of his age group and his behaviour also earned the approval of his elders. He was never known to display excessive emotion, preferred quiet to noise and was spiritual without making a show of his devotions. His talk was coloured by parables and cryptic sayings, which he would let others work out for themselves. He said of his age set, known as *Kaapleelach,* "When the turn of the *Kaapleelach* comes, if they don't die they live," which was interpreted as meaning that his generation would distinguish themselves in battle. Of traitors he would say, "they will eat their own feet," meaning much the same as the English phrase, "they will dig their own graves."

In accordance with his status, he would take six wives, have twenty children and own several homesteads. The Nandi lived in homesteads set some way from one another rather than in conventional villages so that in the Nandi context, village must be taken to refer to a loose concentration of homesteads. The main dwelling of Koitaleel was at *Cheboiin,* a round-walled building made of wood, mud and cow dung with a cone-shaped thatch. He had other homesteads at *Kipriria* and *Kapsimotwo*.

He was already a man when his father was enthroned as chief Oorgoiyoot and Kimnyolei was not ashamed to consult with his son when considering difficult decisions. Through the early years of success, there were many such decisions. Kimnyolei excelled his predecessors in his ability to secure the approval of Heaven for the raiding parties that were necessary-both for adding to the tribal herds and for testing the valour of the young men.

Then, without warning or apparent cause, Assiis turned his face from the Nandi. Whenever the Oorgoiyoot sought divine favour for a raiding party, he would encounter silence or disapproval from the Heavens. Again and again, he was forced to tell the warriors that the time was not yet ripe for them to do battle. The braves were discontented but the remembrance of the fate of those who had defied Kimnyolei by eating the diseased buffalo served to deter them from raiding without his blessing.

Eventually, the Kaptumoiis and the Kapsiondoi, the regiments that had eaten of the diseased buffalo, announced that they would go out with or without the permission of the Oorgoiyoot. Kimnyolei, hearing of their intent, spoke strongly against them and warned that they were courting disaster. They took no heed and set out to battle. Their raid was a complete success, many cattle were captured and no lives were lost. It was a blow to Kimnyolei's reputation but this was soon restored, albeit at a tragic cost. It was found that the captured beasts were riddled with rinderpest, which they passed on to the Nandi herds, killing many cattle and causing great mourning.

The reduction of the Nandi livestock from the rinderpest may have saved Kimnyolei from the accusation that his second sight had failed but it also sowed the seeds of his downfall. As the herds dwindled, the pressure upon the Oorgoiyoot to secure Assiis' blessing for a raid to replenish the people's losses increased. Yet though Kimnyolei sought the will of Heaven with diligence and piety, his God remained silent. He was granted no word or omen that would have allowed him to approve a raiding party. Time and again, the braves would come to him begging for his blessing and, each time, with a heavy heart, he was forced to turn them away.

The young men who were eager to prove themselves in battle grumbled and asked if the job of the Oorgoiyoot was confined to predicting success or failure. Was it not rather to win the approval of Assiis for that which was necessary and right? The old men stroked their beards and spoke of the days of Kimnyolei's father and grandfather, men who had known how to grasp the mandate of Heaven.

To make matters worse, Kimnyolei increasingly talked of matters which the people could not understand and which made them fear for his sanity. He spoke of the coming of the white man, those pale spirits known to the Nandi only by report. These wizards, he said, bred metal beasts that spat fire and could kill companies of men from a great distance with a single roar. Most puzzling of all, he prophesied that a vast iron snake would rip through the land, breathing fire and smoke and ruining all who stood in its path. The fulfilment of this prophecy, he said, would mark the end of the world of the Nandi in the form of the loss of their lands and cattle. He looked forward to his own death, saying that he did not know how long he had left and that Assiis had told him to make use of his time to warn his people of that which was to come.

His words did not please his hearers. They complained that he wasted their time by frightening them with tall tales. In their view, he should have been bending the ear of Heaven to secure the favour of Assiis, that the warriors might be victorious and able to provide for their kin. "Perhaps", they said to themselves, "so much time spent in the realm of the spirits has turned his wits."

It was then that the Kaptumoiis and the Kapsiondoi decided to go raiding again with or without the permission of the Oorgoiyoot. They went to Kimnyolei and demanded he bless them. He informed them that he had no right to speak a word that Heaven had not placed in his mouth and warned them that if they proceeded with their plan, they would lose many lives. The fulfilment of this prophecy did not move the rebels to repentance. They reasoned that they had been forced to take matters into their own hands as a result of Kimnyolei's failure to secure Heaven's blessing and that his refusal to bless them had condemned their comrades to death. Many of those from the other regiments sympathised with the rebels and the murmurs against the Oorgoiyoot grew to a clamour.

Then, just as it looked as if the whole community would end by defying Kimnyolei, he announced that he had joyous news. God had spoken, the time had come. If the warriors went out to battle, the hand of Assiis would be upon them and the ancestors would fight on their side. The people rejoiced and the braves went out in good heart with the expectation of returning with many cattle and much glory. The raiding party consisted of many young men, drawn from all the pororyoosiek of the Nandi.

The raid was a disaster. The Nandi gained nothing and were repulsed by their intended targets, the Luo. Hundreds of braves were massacred, just a handful of men survived to bring the news of the tragedy. As the cries of mourning women spread the news, shock, grief and anger gripped the hearts of the people. How could Kimyolei have failed and sent out the warriors with false words of comfort? Had his second sight deserted him? To answer this question, we are forced to resort to speculation. Is it possible that, faced with a silent Heaven, Kimyolei had grasped at straws and interpreted some chance sign as an omen of victory? Did he perhaps reason that Assiis must wish to bless his people and view the urgency of their needs as sufficient proof of the rightness of the action necessary to supply them?

We can easily imagine how fervently he must have beseeched Assiis and the ancestors, not only for the sake of his position and reputation but also for the welfare of his people. How troubled in spirit he must have felt as the fat melted from their flames and the community's herds continued to dwindle! No longer could raiding be regarded as a sport. It had become a deadly necessity.

It is hard not to sympathise with the position in which Kimyolei had found himself. If he had continued to deny the fighters his blessing, they would certainly have reached the point when they would have chosen to go forth without it. Had they then failed in their mission, he would have been blamed for jinxing it. Had they succeeded, he would have been discredited. How tempting then to feel that the movement of his heart in sympathy with his people was due to the working of the spirit of divination? He must have badly wanted to believe, like so many prophets before and since, that the words his lips longed to speak were also the words of God.

It would seem then that events had proved the Oorgoiyoot a fraud. If he had ever possessed the second sight, it had surely departed from him. Yet we should not be too hasty in judgement. Jewish and Christian readers may think of the words of their common scripture decreeing that those who make a prediction, which does not come to pass are to be regarded as false prophets deserving of death. However, there is another Bible passage which also comes to mind when considering Kimnyolei's story.

We read in the Second book of Chronicles that the Prophet Micah was asked by Ahab, the wicked King of Israel, to prophesy whether the King would crush his enemies if he faced them in battle. "Go up and prosper and they shall be delivered into your hand" was the prophet's first reply. It was only when the King demanded that he speak the truth that he finally spoke the word that the Lord had given him, "I saw all Israel scattered upon the mountains, as sheep that have no shepherd."

This story not only shows that true prophets can fail, it also suggests another possible explanation of the apparent failure of Kimnyolei's second sight. Perhaps he did not mishear the voice of Assiis. It could be that he heard correctly that any raid would fail but was unwilling to deliver the message he received. Seeing that raiding was necessary to the welfare of the people and that they would eventually choose to fight without his blessing should he withhold it, it may be that he decided to stand with his people even against the Heavens. He may have reasoned that if they had to fight, it was better that they should do so with a glad heart and in a state of grace than that they should do so in rebellion against the words of God. He might even have hoped that by withholding these words he could spare his people from guilt and take their sin upon his own head. "Perhaps", he may have said to himself, "Assiis will be moved by the constancy of my prayers or the courage of our warriors and turn his heart once again to his people. And if he does not, it may yet be that the ancestors will take up arms and do battle on behalf of their children."

It was not to be. Neither prayers nor fasting and tears, nor yet the honouring of the ancestors, had been able to turn the will of Heaven. Yet though his powers had failed him, Kimnyolei was enough of a prophet to hear his death song sung in the cries of the mourning women.

Desiring that no one should succeed him as Oorgoiyoot, he took the tools of office and hid them. It is said that he commanded a rock to open and that when he had hidden the tools, the rock closed after them. Then he brewed beer and called all his wives and his children together to tell them that his race was run and that they had to leave him, to flee to the places of safety that he had chosen for them. His family begged him to leave with them and so save his life. Koitaleel's stepmother, Cheepo Kokwarei, was the most insistent, throwing herself at her husband's feet and grasping his legs, wetting his lap with her tears. Kimnyolei would not be moved and demanded that his family submit to his last command, extracting from each in turn a promise of obedience. But when it came to the turn of Cheepo Kokwarei, she threw off the habit of a lifetime and defied her husband.

"My Lord" she said, "all the days of our life together I have obeyed you without question or complaint. When you have called I have come running, if you have sent me away I have not reproached you. But what you ask me now is too great for me. When and where you die, then and there I shall die with you. Where your blood flows, there mine shall mingle with it. And we shall greet the ancestors together."

On hearing these words, Kimnyolei wept. But seeing her mind was made up, he released her from his command saying, "As you have spoken so shall it be".

Then he spoke to his sons, warning them against the Nandi as an ungrateful and rebellious people. "Know this," he said, "Assiis will not hold this people guiltless for my death. If they had humbled themselves and listened to my words of warning, perhaps they could yet have escaped the judgement that is to come. But now my prophecies shall be sealed in blood and God will harden his heart against the Nandi. He will bring against them a cruel nation before whom spears and bows shall be of no avail. The flower of Nandi manhood shall be cut down and seen no more, the people's cattle shall be taken from them and their lands given to strangers. And if any of you should agree to serve them as Oorgoiyoot, from that moment Assiis will put a number on your days and, although you may prosper for a time and a season, your end will come upon you suddenly and those who follow you shall be destroyed."

Despite this prohibition, he passed on the three sacred staffs of the Oorgoiyoot to Koitaleel, which he had retained when he had hidden the other tools of office. Then he commanded his sons to bring him a pure white bull, the finest in his herd, in order that he might sacrifice to the shades of those ancestors he was so shortly to join. The bull, though not drugged, went meekly to the slaughter, greeting its end not with a bellow but with a mournful cry. The Oorgoiyoot pulled the beast's tongue from its mouth and stabbed it with the thorn of an acacia tree, crying as he did so "neither foe nor friend!" prophesying that the Nandi would be driven back in battle and deserted by their allies. When his sons asked him the meaning of his action, he replied that the tongue was the leadership of the Nandi.

"The commanders of the Nandi shall shatter like a pot, and the great men of the Kipsigis like a calabash. If I die in the morning, the people shall perish in the evening!"

Koitaleel, understanding the seriousness of his father's curse, asked if there was not some way of lifting it. Kimnyolei replied,

"When all of my words have been fulfilled and the people have humbled themselves, then the curse may be lifted by a ceremony of sacrifice and the driving of a scapegoat into the wilderness".

For the Nandi, in addition to sharing many common customs with the Jews, also possessed a scapegoating ritual.

He then asked his sons to look into the pot of beer and describe what they saw. His other sons saw nothing, but Koitaleel saw white men with sticks (guns), seeking to climb out of the pot.

"These are those who will kill you if you agree to serve this people", Kimnyolei told him.

After this, his family left him in accordance with his wishes each to the place that he had appointed. And Koitaleel went to Keiyo where his mother's family was.

Kimnyolei then gave his wife a gourd of milk with instructions to sprinkle it towards the East, West and South. Cheepo Kokwarei understood that her husband intended to bless those sections of the Nandi. Coming herself from the North, she felt that her people also deserved a blessing and thus cast the milk in all four directions of the compass. She reasoned that her husband had commanded her to bless the East, West and South, without forbidding her to bless the North. In fact, the scattering of the milk was intended as a curse on those amongst the Nandi that had rebelled. Thus, without intending to, Cheepo Kokwarei helped to curse the whole people. Kimnyolei, not wishing to accuse his wife of disobedience in this last hour, chose instead to believe that Assiis had guided her in order that his full wrath might be poured out upon a disobedient people.

The people, meanwhile, had been discussing the fate of the

Oorgoiyoot. Amongst the Nandi, as amongst the people of Israel, it was decreed that he who prophesied falsely should die. Nevertheless, the regiments were divided. The Kaptumoiis, the Kapsiondoi, the Koilegei and the Kakipooch all spoke for death. The other pororyoosiek felt it would be sacrilegious to strike God's prophet and that judgement should be left to Assiis, albeit without committing themselves to stand against those who might seek to lay hands upon him.

Now the regiment known as Kaptumoiis, which had been cursed by Kimnyolei for the eating of the diseased buffalo, had stored their anger in their hearts since that day. While the Oorgoiyoot yet enjoyed the favour of Heaven, they had kept silent but when they saw that Assiis had turned against him, they determined to seek revenge. Their warriors met with those of the Kapsiondoi to discuss how they would proceed.

The boldest amongst the Kaptumoiis stood before the others and gave voice to the overflow of their bitterness.

"Warriors of the Nandi, comrades and friends! You know that in the days of our ancestors, the people held fast to their liberties. They honoured the Oorgooik, without allowing them to lord it over us. Then came this family of Maasai and with magic arts and winning words, they succeeded in assuming a royal dignity that was not theirs. They made a pact with the people that if we would follow them they would secure for us the favour of Assiis and our enemies would flee before our warriors. Kopogoi and Turugat honoured this pact. Even this Kimnyolei before he became choked with pride was able to lead us to victory. Yet since he cursed our brothers he has himself been cursed by God and now he has sent our comrades to their deaths with false promises ringing in their ears. While he lives, our warriors will continue to be driven back by our enemies and before long the people will perish. Let us rid ourselves of him and cleanse his sins with blood in order that our people should live. The other regiments hesitate to strike, remembering his former powers. But if his blessings are of no effect, why then should we fear his curses? If we kill this man, those who have feared him will praise us as benefactors. And let us destroy his seed also that he shall have no son to succeed him and that we may live as free men!"

His words fell softly on the ears of his hearers and all were agreed that Kimnyolei should die. Thus, they collected *mosigisik*, the two and a half feet throwing sticks sharpened on both sides that the Nandi used for executions and went to seek out the Oorgoiyoot.

They found him sitting on his stool of Eewat wood with his wife squatting a little distance from him. When he saw that his hour had come, Kimnyolei went forward to meet the advancing warriors. Cheepo Kokwarei followed him a few paces behind, not because her courage was less than his but because it was the custom of the people. Some of the men hung back awed by their unnatural calm. But the speaker who had urged Kimnyolei's death strode forward and demanded to know where the Oorgoiyoot had hidden his sons.

"Where you cannot hurt them," came the reply.

The warrior was angered and he threw his sharpened stick at Kimnyolei, cutting open his face. Then the others launched their staves at him until his life force was extinguished.

As for the outrages that were inflicted on Cheepo Kokwarei before her tortured spirit was set free from her broken body, they were so shameful in nature that it would be indecent even to recount them.

Chapter 3

Seeds of the struggle

As A.T. Matson noted in his book, *Nandi Resistance to British Rule*, the territory of the Nandi placed them in an excellent position to dominate their neighbours. They were able to fall upon their victims and take their cattle and then retreat behind a defensive screen of escarpments and forests. The Luo sometimes retaliated with attacks on Nandi settlements below the escarpments but never attempted to raid the Nandi plateau. To strengthen their frontiers at points of vulnerability, the Nandi founded permanently-manned lookout posts on intercommunicating hilltops, a particularly effective measure for a people famed for their ability to see long distances.

Nevertheless, territory alone does not make a race of warriors. Nandi culture was crucial in turning boys into men and men into warriors. Each male was reared from birth to regard himself as a protector of his people. Matson cites games, herding duties, and long journeys to salt licks as means by which boys were trained in self discipline and endurance. The trials involved in coming of age ceremonies also served to strengthen courage and ties of comradeship.

Military exercises were used to maintain fighting fitness and warriors followed a strict diet and abstained from beer and tobacco.

Over time, and even before the appointment of a chief Oorgoiyoot, a system of military command and cooperation was developed. Information gathered by spies and reconnaissance patrols was used to draw up operational plans for raids, which were then submitted for the blessing of the Oorgooik.

To quote Matson, "Several of the raids took only a day to carry out but others took more than a week and necessitated the carrying of rations in the form of stiff porridge and curdled milk…Surprise was essential, since the aggressors were generally outnumbered by the defenders, and fortified positions such as walled and ditched villages and barricaded caves had to be stormed. The Nandi perfected the guerrilla technique of the hit and run attack and usually got away before counter measures could be undertaken by adversaries who were unaccustomed to venture from their homes during the hours of darkness." Nandi prowess in running also assisted in this style of warfare, and to this day, they are known as Kenya's runners.

It would, however, be a slur on the Nandi's courage to imply that they shrank from pitched battle. In their struggle with the Maasai, they fought many such battles and repelled the enemy. They developed the square formation, independently of other armies that used it, as well as the tactic of shooting arrows high to land upon enemies protected by thick bush. In their long-running rivalry with the Uasin Nkishu Maasai, the Nandi gradually prevailed, gaining supremacy over the Uasin Nkishu plateau and assimilating some of the Maasai along the way.

In addition to facing down and defeating neighbouring peoples, the Nandi gained wider fame by their humiliation of the "Arabs" or

"Swahilis" – Muslims of mixed Arab and Swahili heritage who sought to pass through Nandi with their caravans. These were routinely attacked and plundered and the Nandi developed a technique to overcome the advantage possessed by the Arabs in the form of firearms. They would draw the enemy fire with a sudden rush, duck down to avoid the volley then get up and slaughter their opponents before they could reload. This tactic was especially useful in the face of a ragged volley, as the sound of the first shot served as a warning to duck. In the face of a more disciplined enemy wielding more sophisticated firearms, such tactics would prove less useful.

For a time, the Nandi tolerated Arab trading posts in Southern Nandi and did business with them. Then the Arabs, feeling themselves secure, started to abuse the people. The Arabs allowed their donkeys to trample Nandi crops, they poured porridge over one man and flour over another, they tried to imprison some Nandi youths and began to molest Nandi girls and women. As the Arabs could have predicted had they not been blinded by arrogance, the Nandi refused to stand for such treatment. Two of the trading posts were ransacked and their inhabitants massacred, a third was hastily dismantled. Thereafter, the Arabs generally detoured to avoid the Nandi.

Thus, by martial virtue and self discipline, the Nandi had achieved dominance over a sphere of influence extending well beyond their heartlands. In their raiding of other communities, a kind of law of war was acknowledged and women and children were supposed to be spared. Matson says that Nandi elders often ended their narrative by saying that the Nandi withdrew after securing their objectives, having no wish to completely destroy their opponents. Nevertheless, the Nandi used whatever means necessary to secure victory and they rarely had to taste the bitterness of defeat. The people then had some grounds for looking down on others and a Nandi warrior who came of age during the prosperity of Kimnyolei could have been forgiven for feeling that in being born a man of the Nandi, he had drawn first prize in the lottery of life.

The British were another people who felt this way about themselves. Masters of the world's greatest Empire, they were accustomed not to proclaim their superiority but rather to take it for granted. They even succeeded in persuading themselves that they acted from substantially altruistic motives. In contrast, say, to the excuses made by the Belgians for the Congo genocide, Britain's conceit about her civilising mission cannot be dismissed as pure hypocrisy. The suppression of the slave trade, for example, was a real achievement and it won't do to say that those who spent their lives in this cause were not sincere. Nor are the achievements of the anti-slavers diminished by the consideration that the British naval dominance necessary to stop the slave trade also served the interests of the commercial class whose support was crucial to any campaign hopeful of success. Few reforms succeed without enlisting the support of powerful, and at least partly self-interested, allies.

The substantial suppression of the overseas slave trade did not spell the end of the campaign against the trade. Slavery remained widespread in the interior of Africa and slave caravans by far the most economical way of transporting goods across the continent. Evangelical anti-slavers, therefore, moved to demanding action against Africa's internal slave trade, working in close alliance with Christian missionaries who wanted Britain to help them open up the "dark continent" to the light of the gospel. Thus, Britain's part in the "Scramble for Africa" – the expansion of European empires into the African interior – secured the support of the "do gooding" as well as the commercial classes, two groups that substantially overlapped. The desire of businessmen to get their hands on African minerals and lands may be seen as an essential engine of colonial expansion but in the case, at least, of British Africa, it cannot be portrayed as the only motor force. The British, if not the Belgians, took seriously the civilising mission that the English author and poet, Rudyard Kipling, called "the white man's burden."

There were also strategic considerations moving the British state to support her merchants and missionaries. British statesmen had become much exercised by the notion that if any other power secured control of the headwaters of the Nile, they would be able to dam them and to destroy the prosperity of Egypt. Sir Evelyn Baring, the future Lord Cromer and British Consul in Cairo stated: "Were a civilised power established in the Nile Valley they could so reduce the water supply as to ruin the country...Whatever power holds the Upper Nile Valley must by mere force of its geographical situation dominate Egypt." Moreover, Egypt with its Suez Canal was the lynchpin of the British Empire so these fears conjured up the spectre of a threat to Britain's global dominance.

Such imaginings look feverish in retrospect. Any power desirous of cutting off the Nile would first have had to conquer the territories containing the source of the Nile's tributaries. Then they would have had to spend many years and vast resources on the necessary engineering. The accomplishment of such a plan might have been within the outer limits of the capability of another European power but only if Britain had chosen to sit back and do nothing while all this was going on. In the real world, the extended timeline of any such project would have made it easy for Britain to squash and thus pointless for any rival to attempt. Yet such nightmares were as influential as any commercial considerations in prompting the British to secure control of Uganda.

This occurred in 1888, one year after the British had gained control of Mombasa. To many, it seemed that the next logical step would be to create a railway that would connect Uganda with Mombasa and allow its more effective exploitation. This idea was embraced not only by businessmen but, at least as enthusiastically, by anti-slavers. They correctly guessed that the projected railway would spell the beginning of the end of slavery in Africa by putting the slave caravans out of business.

This alliance of administrators, adventurers and idealists made quick headway and plans began to be drawn up for the Kenya-Uganda Railway that would be nicknamed, as a result of its spectacular cost overruns and numerous setbacks, "The Lunatic Express".

The evangelists for this project knew that the line would have to cut through difficult territory inhabited by warlike peoples. From the limited information initially available, it was the Maasai that were most feared. As more information was gathered, it would become clear that the Nandi were likely to constitute at least as great an obstacle.

Yet these looming threats struck no fear into the hearts of the railway boosters. Other peoples no less martial had been humbled by British arms. King Cetewayo of the Zulu had been the heir to Chaka, the "black Alexander", but his crown had been taken from him nonetheless. The prevailing British sentiment with regard to wars with "native" peoples was that summed up by the poet Hilaire Belloc a few years later: "Whatever happens we have got. The Maxim gun, and they have not."

Even the most optimistic, however, could not have hoped that the opening up of the Nandi lands and its sphere of influence would go as smoothly as it initially did. In the years after Kimnyolei's death in 1890, these territories would be crossed not only by a railway survey party but by an increasing number of European-led caravans. By the end of 1894, 45 European caravans had crossed the Nandi sphere of influence. Another 40 caravans would pass through in the first half of

1895 alone. Yet the same people who had refused to allow the Arabs through their territory except by permission and with the payment of bribes, sat back and watched as the white locusts gathered to devour their land. An attempt was made to extract gifts from one caravan but no reprisal had been taken when the demand was rebuffed. Even the construction, in 1894, of a British fort at Ravine on the edge of Nandi lands passed without provoking a reaction. The only significant trouble from the Nandi was a solitary attack on the headman of a caravan who had fallen behind the rest to help a sick porter. Though wounded, he escaped alive, testimony, as Matson says, to the fact that his attackers were neither numerous nor determined.

Such serious resistance as the British did encounter came from other peoples, notably the "Kitosh" (Bukusu) who, in December 1894, cut to pieces a large party that had supposed itself to be under the protection of the nascent British administration. As for the Nandi, it seemed that they had been exposed as paper tigers who could be cowed into submission by a superior enemy.

The final insult to Nandi pride was delivered by one Andrew Dick, an entrepreneur seeking to establish a chain of stores and transport posts from the Coast to Lake Victoria. Dick had drifted to Kenya from South Africa, where he had been expelled from the Cape Mounted Rifles for gun running. By June 1895, he was leading a caravan through Nandi country. His trek had started badly when three of his rifles had been looted. Meanwhile, the herd of cattle he had sent ahead of his caravan had been stampeded by lions on the Uasin Nkishu plateau. Thus, Dick was in an inhospitable mood when his camp by the Kipkarren river was approached by two Nandi men bearing grass in their hands as a sign of peace. The Nandi asked for food, saying that they were starving. Dick ordered his headman to tie them both up and give them each a hundred strokes with a rawhide whip. He also had them interrogated in the Maasai language to see if they had anything to do with the theft of his guns or the disappearance of his cattle. They denied both charges but admitted that other Nandi men had rounded up Dick's cattle. When Dick demanded they lead him to the homes of the thieves, the men claimed not to know where they lived. They were tied to a tree for the night, and in the morning, they were thrown into the river with their hands and legs bound. Both drowned.

As Dick's caravan was breaking camp, he saw a group of Nandi warriors spying from a distance and fired three times, wounding one. The rest of his trip was without incident and he went his way feeling, no doubt, that he had taught the "natives" a jolly good lesson. He had. He showed any Nandi still capable of doubting it that the white man was even more arrogant than the Arabs, who had at least waited until they were protected by fortifications before lording it over them.

The price of Dick's folly was to be paid by his trading partner, West. West was a very different type of man from Dick. Dick regarded black Africans as brutes, West treated them as men. He had befriended some Nandi and had sworn blood brotherhood with one of their chiefs, apparently ignorant of the fact that this was not a custom native to the Nandi. Thus, he had no reason to expect trouble when he followed in Dick's footsteps across Nandi, being unaware of the havoc his partner had wrought.

Feeling himself secure, West made no effort to fortify the camp that he pitched in a wood below the West escarpment as a base for trading with the local people. This was a fatal miscalculation. On 16th July 1895, West's camp was overrun by Nandi warriors who stabbed their spears through the tents before any shots could be fired by the occupants. West and most his people were slaughtered, though eight managed to escape.

What proved remarkable about this incident was not so much

that the Nandi had finally roused themselves and taken vengeance for the abuse they had suffered but that West's murder proved to be just the opening act of a Nandi war of resistance that would extend for almost eleven years and unite the regiments against the British. How was it possible that a people who for five years had been paralysed by division and fear, should so suddenly come together and gird themselves once again for war?

Chapter 4

Confounding the British Empire

"In the days when all the parts of the human body were not as now agreeing together, but each member took its own course and spoke its own speech, the other members, indignant at seeing that everything by their care and labour and ministry went to the belly, whilst it, undisturbed in the middle of them all did nothing but enjoy the pleasures provided for it, entered into a conspiracy; the hands were not to bring food to the mouth, the mouth was not to accept it when offered, the teeth were not to chew it. Whilst, in their resentment they were anxious to coerce the belly by starving it, the members themselves wasted away and the whole body was reduced to the last stage of exhaustion. Then it became evident that the belly rendered no idle service and the nourishment it received was no greater than that which it bestowed ..."

Livy, History of Rome

The death of Kimnyolei did not have the effect that his murderers had hoped for. Far from initiating a new era of freedom and self government, it tore the people apart. Many who had wished for his death recoiled when the deed was done. When they heard of the slaying of God's prophet and the sadistic and impious violation of his wife, a great fear of Heaven's judgement gripped their hearts. And those not bound to the killers by close ties of kith and kin drew back from them in horror.

Thus, when Kimnyolei's prophecies began to come true in the form of the British encroachment into Nandi, the people watched and quarrelled but took no action. Raiding of other communities continued but united action against the new enemy was paralysed by the divisions between the regiments and the demoralisation of the people. Meanwhile, rinderpest continued unabated and famine and smallpox followed hard on the heels of Kimnyolei's death.

The Nandi had never been able to field a great army, possessing no more than a few thousand active warriors even at their peak, but the regimental system and the martial spirit of the people had enabled them to cast a shadow out of all proportion to their size. Now that spirit had been broken and the Nandi looked like easy prey for a power like the British.

Then the people remembered their triumphs under Kimnyolei and forgot his failures, mourning bitterly for the leader they had lost. They also remembered the son of his loins who had been distinguished from birth by so many marks of God's favour. If only Koitaleel could be persuaded to take his father's place, perhaps the Nandi might yet rise again.

Thus, the elders of the regiments that had been innocent of Kimnyolei's death met together and agreed to send an ambassador to Keiyo where Koitaleel had fled. The journey would be dangerous as it involved passing through the territory of the hostile Maasai. It was decided that the ambassador should, therefore, disguise himself as a woman, carrying gourds as if on a visit. Amongst the Nandi, as in most patriarchal societies, a man who dresses as a woman invites ridicule. Yet the ambassador chosen, one Mariich, did not hesitate to agree to humble himself for the sake of his people.

We do not know the exact words that he used to persuade Koitaleel to agree to lead his people. We may be sure though, that he gave a full account of the suffering of the Nandi and of their desire for Koitaleel's return. Koitaleel must have had to think hard before agreeing to go back to Nandi. On the one hand, he had to weigh his dying father's commands, a sacred trust for the son of a family distinguished by its reverence for its ancestors. On the other pan of the scale, he had to place the anguish of his people and their need for a shepherd. It is unlikely he believed that any amount of propitiation of his father's spirit would suffice to unloose a curse that had been written in blood. Nevertheless, he may have reasoned that by bequeathing him the sacred staffs, rather than hiding them with the other tools of office, Kimnyolei had left open the option that Koitaleel might succeed him, albeit at the cost of his life. In the end, he seems to have concluded that if the sunset of the people's world had come, he nevertheless could not sit back in peace and safety and watch the shadows devour it. If the Nandi were to be destroyed, it was better that they should pass into the night as fallen warriors than as fleeing cowards and better too that he should die alongside them as their leader than live on as a traitor. And perhaps also Koitaleel, like his father before him, yet hoped to turn the will of Heaven.

On his return, he found that a majority of the regiments were eager for war but that some yet held back. Those that had killed his father were reluctant to accept his leadership, others hoped for peace.

Until 1899, the peace party looked to Koitaleel's brother, Kipchomber, who had also returned from exile and who favoured a more cautious approach. However, precisely because of this, Kipchomber was not a rival for the position of war leader. In 1899, Kipchomber accepted the position of Oorgoiyoot to the Kipsigis, removing himself from the scene and making way for the whole people to unite around Koitaleel.

Koitaleel wasted no time in establishing a line of command and re-establishing the centralised spy system necessary to organise an effective military campaign. He took a personal interest in intelligence work and interviewed a Swahili survivor of the attack on West's camp. The Swahili reported that the Oorgoiyoot preserved a tin of corned beef with great veneration. Koitaleel followed up the first attack with another on a caravan carrying material for a steamship, the "William Mackinnon". The caravan was a substantial one, including two European mechanics, twenty Indian artisans and more than 400 porters. Over twenty loads were lost as a result of the Nandi attack, which demonstrated that even large caravans were not safe. Thereafter, the Nandi were almost continually active and any caravan passing through their territory was liable to be attacked. Not every attack was planned in advance by Koitaleel, some were opportunistic but it was Koitaleel's leadership that fanned the flames of the spreading resistance movement.

The British responded with a punitive expedition led by Major Cunningham and Captain Sitwell, each leading a column into Nandi from different directions hoping to pen the community between the two forces, which totalled more than four hundred (mainly Sudanese) soldiers and hundreds more porters and camp followers. Each column had a Maxim gun and the troops had recently been equipped with Martini-Henry rifles.

Major Cunningham's column succeeded in provoking a pitched battle with the Nandi at Kimondi. 500 Nandi men suddenly appeared over the top of a hill, advancing rapidly and formed into three sides of a square, their spears glinting in the sunlight. The British troops opened fire with rifles and Maxim gun striking down many warriors. But the Nandi kept on coming! Undeterred by the hail of bullets, they continued to advance on the British forces and came close to overwhelming them. The warriors who broke through to the British lines were inspired to a terrifying ferocity by the thought of all those braves who had fallen by the way before they could get within striking range. Thus, for example, brave Sergeant Chongo fell with his scarlet tunic rent in many places and dyed a yet darker shade of red where the Nandi had washed their spears in his blood. The British were saved from defeat only by the courage and discipline of their Sudanese troops, who stood firm and continued firing until the Nandi were finally driven back. A hundred Nandi men were left dead in the field but the British lost fourteen soldiers and two porters.

From the British point of view, this was dangerously close to a defeat. In their wars with African peoples, Britain's superior firepower was supposed to mow down the enemy before they came close enough to strike. Rifles and Maxim guns had a range far exceeding that of spear and arrow and the infliction of heavy casualties on hostile peoples was supposed to break and scatter them. The casualties suffered by their enemies could exceed those of the British-commanded troops by more than a hundred to one. Thus, at the battle of Omdurman in 1898, Britain lost 47 men while killing 10,000 of the enemy. That the Nandi killed sixteen of Cunningham's men was a tribute to Nandi bravery and discipline. The courage of the Nandi made a profound impression on the Sudanese troops and their British officers.

Undeterred by their losses, the Nandi attacked Cunningham's camp at dawn a few days later but were unable to penetrate the five-foot high thorn enclosure and the attack was finally repulsed by repeated volleys from the Sudanese. The Nandi, however, were unbowed and continued to harass the expedition.

Captain Sitwell's column encountered similarly determined resistance. At one point, the Nandi succeeded in breaking into his camp, killing three and wounding five before they were driven off. Both columns suffered persistent attacks with arrows as well as frontal assaults. Their achievement was to kill some number of Nandi men, to burn some huts and crops and to capture some cattle and food supplies. The British, thereby, succeeded in inflicting significant misery on the Nandi, but it was far from a victory.

Throughout the decade-long Nandi resistance, the British believed that the courage of the Nandi was inspired by Koitaleel's promise that his magic would protect them from British bullets. It seems extremely unlikely that he offered any such unconditional pledge. Had he done so, he would have lost authority the first time the promise was exposed as hollow. More likely, he claimed that his charms would increase their chances of survival. The real magic of the Oorgoiyoot was that he awakened in the Nandi breasts their passion for liberty and caused them to put aside tribal disputes to unite in defence of their homeland.

The campaign taught each side to respect the other. The British knew that the Nandi could not be overawed as easily as some other African peoples. The Nandi learnt that the British were an enemy in a different league from the Arabs and the Maasai. Thus, Koitaleel ordered a change of tactics after these experiences. Massed charges were abandoned; camps attacked only after spies had determined that they were vulnerable and raids and ambushes targeted detached parties and stragglers or columns passing through territory where the Nandi could conceal themselves and the British were hampered from retaliation. In short, conventional warfare gave way to a guerrilla strategy.

It had been expected that the campaign would conclude with a beaten people suing for peace and willing to accept British rule. The Nandi's neighbours had expected to see Nandi tribal elders being escorted to Mumias, the town to the West of Nandi controlled by the British, and forced to sign a treaty of submission. When this didn't happen, British prestige was greatly damaged. The Nandi had offered to negotiate at one point in the campaign but they had impudently demanded to be treated as equals and had made clear that surrendering their freedom was not on the agenda.

Amazingly, the British did treat the Nandi as equals in the aftermath of the inconclusive campaign. Certain elders of the community approached the British in Ravine and agreed to seek to restrain their warriors from attacking caravans passing through their territory in return for being left alone by the British. It was an informal truce rather than a peace treaty and its terms were of a kind that would normally be offered to a sovereign state rather than a subject people. Though the British did not surrender their claim to Nandi, they nevertheless refrained from pressing it.

The British did not treat the Nandi's neighbours with the same deference and acted to strengthen their hold over other communities more easily cowed by shows of force. This created the potential for further conflict with the Nandi if they continued to raid the peoples who had been taken under British protection. The British exercised their control from Ravine and from Kipture Fort, also on the edge of Nandi territory. Kipture, which was later replaced by Fort Kaptumo, itself, replaced a fort that had been sited at Kipkarren but which had been destroyed by Nandi warriors before it had been completed.

The peace that followed the unsuccessful British campaign held for most of 1896. The Nandi left the British alone even when they started to build a road to replace the caravan track. Yet the truce turned out to be merely a pause in hostilities. Koitaleel did not believe that the British would rest content with passing through Nandi and leaving its people alone. He was convinced that the British coveted the rich lands of the Nandi and their neighbours.

He was right! As early as 1893, one William Fitzgerald had described the lands of British East Africa as "...a wonderfully fertile country only awaiting the advent of English energy, capital and enterprise for its development..."

Fifteen years later, when white settlement was in full swing, Winston Churchill wrote of his journey on the Kenya-Uganda Railway,

"I will confess that, travelling through the East African Highlands for the first time in my life, I have learnt what the sensation of land hunger is like. We may repress, but we cannot escape, the desire to peg out one of these fair and wide estates, with all the rewards they offer to industry and inventiveness in the open air."

These views were representative of the attitude of Europeans towards the land of Kenya and Uganda. To reach its full potential, they reasoned, it needed to be placed in the hands of whites.

The desire of Europeans to dispossess the local peoples was founded not only on the notion that whites should own the land but also on the belief that blacks shouldn't. The science of economics taught that human beings were rational economic creatures motivated by a desire to enrich themselves. Unfortunately for this theory, indigenous peoples did not appear to behave rationally from the point of view of economists. Economists said that to increase the supply of labour, an employer should increase the price of labour – wages. However, if one doubled an indigenous worker's pay he might halve the number of days he was willing to work. Having few artificial needs, he worked until he had enough to satisfy his natural needs and, thereafter, took his leisure. Moreover, those who had enough land to supply these needs could not be induced to work at all. If they were to be made to work for Europeans, they had to be dispossessed.

This outcome was precisely what Koitaleel was determined to prevent. He had been moving to make contact with other communities putting aside past quarrels in the interest of driving out the invader. By reaching out to other Kenyan peoples in the cause of resisting the British, Koitaleel might be said to have anticipated the idea of Kenya. From this perspective, Koitaleel could be regarded, if not as the first Kenyan then as the true father of Kenya. The first fruits of this anti-colonial alliance was seen on 3rd December 1896, when two of the Uasin Nkishu Maasai who had settled near Ravine and had been granted British protection were killed by "Lembus" – the British name for the members of the Tugen people living in the Eldama Ravine area. Five days later, two hundred Lembus killed six Uasin Nkishu and stole fifty cattle. Two days before Christmas, the Uasin Nkishu settlement at the foot of the hill below Fort Ravine was burnt down. Fifty eight cattle and 500 sheep and goats were looted. Tragically, in addition to the two warriors who died, two women with babies burned to death.

The last outrage involved Nandi as well as Lembus warriors and one of the six attackers who were killed was a Nandi. Another was wounded and both he and nine of the looted stock were subsequently seen in Nandi.

Things heated up further in the New Year. Four Sudanese soldiers carrying mail through Nandi from Kipture to Ravine were attacked in their camp, one man and a girl were killed and the mail stolen. A few days later, thirty government troops were attacked by a large band of warriors. The warriors were repulsed, losing one of their number and a Martini-Henry rifle, which they had captured during the attack on the mail party. Nevertheless, the attack showed that, once again, Nandi had become unsafe to travel through and those willing to brave the risk had to be accompanied by armed escorts.

In March, the Uasin Nkishu captured five head of cattle being driven by a party of Lembus warriors. They were part of the loot from the raid on the Maasai settlement and intended as a reward to Koitaleel for the Nandi's help. Shortly afterwards, the acting Commissioner at Kipture, F.J. Jackson, wrote the following about the restlessness of the local peoples:

"…the great cause of the trouble is the hostile attitude assumed by the Chief Lybon, or medicine man, against the government. This man, who apparently has enormous influence over various surrounding tribes, has declared war against the government and is now busying himself in exhorting the tribes to expel the English. From reliable native information received, I find he is endeavouring to bring about a combined movement against the Administration, and numerous minor pieces of information clearly indicate that combined hostile action against us will undoubtedly begin on the cessation of the present rainy season."

British fears of a general uprising led to the military campaign that became known as the second Nandi expedition, though it was directed not just against the Nandi but also against allied peoples such as the Kipsigis, the Lembus and the Elgeiyo. Nevertheless, the showpiece action of the campaign was intended to be the capture of the mysterious "Lybon" or Laibon, known to his own people as the Oorgoiyoot.

The British undertook a night time march designed to bring them within striking distance of Koitaleel's residence without raising the alarm. The plan went awry as the British were delayed by the difficult terrain and did not arrive till the sun was up. They emerged to look down on the Meteitei Valley, where the people could be seen moving about and their herds grazing. To that extent, the Nandi had been taken by surprise but the scouts posted in the lookouts 1,000 feet above the valley sounded the alarm. The cattle were rapidly rounded up and spirited away. Koitaleel escaped with his cattle leaving the British clutching at shadows.

No cowardice was involved in the Oorgoiyoot's flight. Koitaleel had long before established his courage and daring. On his return from exile, he had, therefore, felt no need to lead from the front. Not for him the vanity of an Alexander, exposing himself and his cause to maximum danger in order that it should be said that he was always in the thick of the battle. Rather, he took care not to risk his life needlessly, knowing that without him the people would be a broken reed. He acted as the brains rather than the right arm of the uprising, sifting information and planning to ensure the success of Nandi tactics.

Koitaleel justified the confidence his people had placed in him by his ability to learn from his mistakes. He avoided the kind of pitched battle that the Nandi had attempted during the previous campaign, realising that a frontal assault gave the advantage to the British and their rifles and Maxim guns. Indeed, during the second Nandi expedition, he encouraged his people to hide from the enemy that they might live another day. If an opportunity for an ambush presented itself, it should be seized but having hit the ambushers, the warriors should run and save their skins. Once the British had returned to their bases, the people could then emerge and resume their normal lives.

The success of this guerrilla tactic was almost complete. The Nandi only killed eight of the enemy but their own casualties were of a similar order. The British managed to capture some cattle and food supplies as before but most of the Nandi herds and flocks escaped.

Other communities were deterred by the British action and the punishment imposed upon them but the Nandi were still standing and defiant. Once again, this small people had faced down the vast British Empire.

This was in many ways Koitaleel's finest campaign. He had discovered the secret of the guerrilla, that an enemy's strength can be used against him and that the avoidance of battle can serve as a form of victory. Thus, the people were content to let the British blunder around their lands, constantly fearful of ambush and counting themselves lucky if they could capture enough cattle to feed themselves. Koitaleel's tactic of hiding from the main body of the enemy and striking only at isolated units negated the British advantage of technological superiority while making maximum use of his people's own assets, their knowledge of the territory, their keenness of eye and their fleetness of foot.

Sadly, the usefulness of the tactic of evasion would diminish over time. The British were assiduous mapmakers, surveyors and intelligence gatherers. With each year that passed, their knowledge of the geography of Nandi increased and the ability of the Nandi to hide very large bodies of people and cattle diminished. In the face of such a determined enemy, guerrilla tactics could deny outright victory to the invaders and ensure that they also suffered loss but they could not prevent the slaughter of some thousands of people, not only warriors, but also women, children and old men. Thus, the British actions against the Nandi and other East African peoples between 1902 and 1906 killed 2,426 persons according to (suspiciously precise) British figures. One notes that the official figures refer to verified deaths, and thus, must be considered base figures. The Nandi have a clear recollection of various British actions that either produced a higher death toll than the British claimed or which went altogether unreported by the colonial authorities.

Insofar as the British figures are understated, it is most likely with regard to these later actions. Between the first Nandi campaign of 1895 and the final campaign of 1905, a sea of change took place in the attitude of the British public towards colonial wars. As late as the battle of Omdurman in 1898, a mountain of enemy corpses could still be seen as a cause for rejoicing. However, the same battle elicited an early expression of the more humane attitude to war that would become commonplace when Kitchener was criticised for killing enemy wounded. By 1905, the revulsion against Belgian genocide in the Congo and Britain's own atrocities against the Boers had caused bloodlust to fall out of fashion. Then it was felt that the best victory was one achieved with the minimum of casualties on either side. Thus, whereas in the earlier actions the British would have been keen to count every corpse, the incentive during the later actions would have been towards understatement.

We cannot be certain of the true total of Nandi killed by the British over the course of five campaigns and five police actions, though we know it ran to several thousands. This is without counting the very large numbers that perished as a result of British seizure of their cattle and destruction of their food stores. The British put the number of cattle seized in the actions of 1902-6 at 93,546, a huge blow to the Nandi and their allies, even before considering the destruction of vast numbers of food stores. Such collective punishments are now forbidden by the law of war, but then they were state policy. The number of Nandi who perished from famine and disease as a result of the loss of food stores and cattle and the infections brought by the railway work camps could well have exceeded 10,000 over the eleven-year period of the conflict. To put this in perspective, the entire adult male population of the Nandi was 10,000 in 1914. Koitaleel keenly felt the suffering of the people and the many deaths from hunger and diseases that would normally have been non-fatal. Nevertheless, not only the Oorgoiyoot but also the body of the people considered that it was better to be hungry and free than well fed slaves.

In 1897, however, the slight British knowledge of Nandi limited their ability to track down people and cattle and allowed the Nandi to hide from the worst of the Empire's wrath. The inconclusive campaign did not force the British to surrender their claim to Nandi but it did persuade them to leave the people alone for some time while they concentrated on consolidating their grip on the surrounding communities and areas. For two years, the two sides felt able to leave each other alone, but all this time the railway was coming closer to Nandi. Hearing reports of the railroad's progress, the people had no doubt that they were seeing the fulfilment of Kimnyolei's prophecy of the iron snake. This brought both the Nandi and their Oorgoiyoot to a crisis point. The people had to decide whether to move from non-cooperation to active resistance when the railway reached Nandi. As for Koitaleel, if he led the resistance, he was effectively committing himself to an attempt to frustrate the fulfilment of his father's prophecy.

The Oorgooik have been called ancestor worshippers. This is incorrect; they were monotheists. However, they certainly venerated their ancestors and thus, Koitaeel was faced with an acute dilemma. If he succeeded in his mission, he would be exposing his father for a second time to the charge of false prophecy; if he failed, the Nandi would cease to exist as a sovereign people.

Perhaps the Oorgoiyoot sought to appease his father's spirit by promising that if Kimnyolei would join in praying for the curse to be lifted, then Koitaleel would ensure that the people knew the source of their deliverance. Perhaps, on the other hand he felt that the curse was unbreakable but that he should, nevertheless, seek to delay its fulfilment. In either case, Koitaleel must have consulted his father's spirit and we may presume that he believed that Kimnyolei did not oppose his course. His father had, after all, devoted his life to the wellbeing of the people and whatever words he had spoken in the bitterness of his last hours, Koitaleel may have felt that Kimnyolei would not condemn him for seeking to save the Nandi.

In this struggle, Koitaleel was prepared to use any means he considered necessary, whether natural or supernatural. Thus, Koitaleel conjured up the totem of the Talai clan, the lion spirit and spoke as follows:

"Brother Lion, as you fought for my ancestor Kopogoi, now fight for me! Descend upon our nation's foes and rend their flesh, that they might be terrified and turn back!"

And British history records that at Tsavo, more than 100 railway workers were consumed by man-eating lions.

Yet the British did not believe in spells, trusting instead in the magic of the .303 Lee Enfield and the Martini-Henry. The threat that had been raised by the Oorgoiyoot's incantations was laid to rest by military science and the lions of Tsavo went the way of the Empire's other enemies.

Koitaleel fretted that his prayers could not stop the British and it is said that at a certain point in the conflict, he decided that he needed a skull of a white man in order to give his curses greater power. Jacob Chumba, formerly acting Kenyan ambassador to the Democratic Republic of the Congo, relates the following story from oral sources. Koitaleel summoned two sharpshooters, araap Kuna and araap Siirtui and commissioned them to seek out a white man and bring him the head. They travelled for a very great distance, but the only white men they spied were protected by large companies. Eventually, they came upon a white man protected by just two "Nubians", the Nandi term for the black African soldiers who served the British, as a result of the many Sudanese amongst them. The sharpshooters' first pair of arrows felled the Nubians, the second struck down the white man, whose head they took.

On the long march home, the weight of the head became irksome and it was agreed that the head should be roasted in order that the flesh could be removed, as the Oorgoiyoot needed only the skull. Since the men had not eaten for a considerable time and had no supplies, the sweet smell of the roasting meat tickled their nostrils and caused their mouths to water. It should be understood here that the Nandi were never cannibals, yet in this case hunger overcame the men's scruples and they decided to eat the white man's flesh. The Nandi custom was that a returning warrior should announce "I come from war!" and stay apart from the people until they had been ceremonially cleansed of guilt for all acts of war. Thus, araap Kuna and araap Siirtui could look forward to absolution for their deed, and perhaps also reasoned that white men were devils rather than human beings and that eating their flesh did not constitute cannibalism.

The British, so the tale goes, sent spies on the heels of the sharpshooters. Having learnt of their story, they spread the word that, far from being angry, they were so impressed by the marksmanship of the two men that they wished to honour them. If they came forward they would be given a herd of 100 cattle. Araap Kuna and Siirtui were suspicious, but 100 cattle was a fortune and they decided to take the risk and show themselves to the British, who seized and detained them.

Whatever curse Koitaleel effected using this skull, it did not succeed in stopping the "white devils". The British had decided to route their railway through the valley to the South of Nandi. This meant that the Nandi heartlands would be sandwiched between, on the one hand, the road that the British had built and the telegraph they planned, and on the other, the projected railroad. Moreover, the valley contained a large Nandi population. The Nandi, still weak from the effects of smallpox and rinderpest had perhaps 2,000 or so active warriors they could field. Nevertheless, they did not shrink from the coming confrontation, being willing to make any sacrifice to safeguard their freedom.

So Koitaleel rallied the people to stand once again against the British. His brother Kipchomber had then removed himself to serve as Oorgoiyoot to the Kipsigis, allowing the people to unite around Koitaleel's leadership. Kipchomber appears to have disapproved of his brother's defiance of their father's command while also resenting the fact that the throne had not been offered to him as the first born. Nevertheless, he seems to have winked at collaboration between Kipsigis militants and the Nandi.

The Nandi campaign was launched with an attack on a group of railway workers. Further attacks on both the railroad and the telegraph followed. The telegraph wire was carried off and turned into jewellery, railway sleepers were stolen and used to make pots and spearheads. Constant raids stalled progress on the railway and telegraph and closed the Nandi territory to travellers.

Ronald Hardy, in *The Iron Snake*, quotes a European foreman to illustrate the troubles faced by the workers who laid the telegraph:

"They (the Nandi) had eyes like eagles and nothing escaped them for long. I wondered what went on in their minds as they saw men diligently uncoiling wire through the country at a height of twenty five feet above the ground. Now there is one thing that sends a howling savage into transports of delight – and that is a length of wire line.

They stole miles of it. At first they waited for us to lay it, descending at night and removing it. Then they saved themselves the trouble and conceived a plan of attacking the parties before the wire was uncoiled. The coolies were terrified. They ate their chop grovelling on their bellies in the undergrowth. One day we came on a dead Punjaubi (sic) up a pole near to the Kedowa Stream. They had filled him full of arrows and he was hanging there like a dead bird. After that the coolies refused to work until the district had been thoroughly scouted …"

A militia had to be formed to protect the workers, making use of anyone who could use a rifle, from Sikhs to Baluchis, Swahilis, Zanzibaris and others. Command was given to former caravan master, Robert Turk. This militia was also used during the 1900 campaign against the Nandi, which was made necessary by the same constant warfare that had led to the unit's formation.

In the early days of this campaign, the Nandi were again able to frustrate their enemy by hiding. Then the British had a stroke of luck. Ronald Hardy records that they encountered a vast herd of cattle representing perhaps half the wealth of the Nandi people and protected by just thirty warriors. These herdsmen were easily slaughtered by Maxim gun fire with the exception of four who succeeded in escaping. Then, rather than rounding up the cattle, the British decided to slaughter the herds. The non-white troops had no idea why their officers commanded such an act. It was one thing to steal the Nandi cattle, quite another to senselessly slaughter them. Yet the soldiers obeyed their orders and the valley was filled with the piteous bellowing of the doomed beasts.

The Nandi were incensed by the murder of their beloved cattle, which they learnt of from the herdsmen that had escaped the massacre. The policy of caution was thrown to the winds in the service of revenge. That night, an attack was launched on the camp of another British column. The Nandi, alongside Kipsigis allies, fought with a bravery and ferocity bordering on insanity, displaying complete indifference to the hail of British bullets from Maxim gun and rifle, leaving three quarters of the column dead or wounded. The cattle that the column had captured were liberated.

This was not the end of the British misery. The expeditionary force suffered numerous other casualties. Then the Nandi had wiped out a platoon of twenty Sudanese soldiers, not part of the expeditionary force, which had been left behind to protect the mail. Worst of all, the British found that Koitaleel had escaped them again, although at one point in the campaign he had been reported killed. In short, the campaign was a disaster. The British offered another truce, which the Nandi accepted, but without signing the treaty the British originally proposed. The tribal leaders, with Koitaleel's blessing, promised only to keep the peace, implying equality between the British and the Nandi. The British decided that a policy of appeasement was to be preferred to fruitless wars at least until the railway had been completed.

Thus, gifts were given to selected Nandi leaders and provocations ignored. Ronald Hardy records that numerous attacks were made upon the Indian labourers ("coolies") in revenge for the kidnapping of numbers of Nandi women and children. Workers were seized, mutilated and hung on the thorns of the *bomas*. Entire gangs were murdered, sometimes buried alive.

Yet in keeping with the policy of appeasement, the British turned a blind eye to such incidents. Skirmishes were recorded as 'parleys', battles as 'disputes', casualties and deaths as losses to 'disease.'

The British, hoping to placate the Nandi, moved to remedy a great grievance that affected not only the Nandi but also other local peoples.

The women and children the Indian workers had kidnapped had been put to use as sex slaves. Such an outrage would have roused the anger of any people, let alone a proud nation such as the Nandi. The British, hardly less shocked than the local communities by the depravity of the "coolies", determined to take action. Robert Turk entered the workmen's camp with twenty militiamen to rescue the sex slaves. Turk's impressions are recorded by Ronald Hardy:

"Went in the middle of morning when Indos were out at work…. We went through that place with a comb, tent to tent, rousing out the whores …we took Nandi girls and some Lumbwa and Wa-kamasie and a whole lot of little boys and girls the Indos had been at, it made you cry to see them."

The return of these lost souls to the bosoms of their kith and kin had the opposite effect to that which the British had intended. Those who had formerly been able to dismiss reports of their loved ones' fates as rumour and to hope that their enslaved wives and children might at least have been put to honest toil now had their darkest fears confirmed. Learning of the vile indecencies that had been forced upon the women and children merely fanned the flames of the people's anger.

It is, therefore, unsurprising that this truce went the way of the others and that the Nandi resumed their attacks on the railway. In 1902, they raided Kibigori station and stole 30 steel sleepers, exceeding their former depredations. Shortly afterwards, their Kipsigis kin raided the construction camps killing and wounding coolies. In 1903, the most militant of the Nandi regiments, the Kamelilo, took the resistance yet further, carrying off 1,000 "dog spikes" from one camp and 800 rivets from another. Thereafter, they removed 30 fish plates in broad daylight, following up this feat by an attack on a Somali trader. These and other outrages prompted the British to launch another expedition, which lasted five weeks and ended with the British proclaiming a victory despite their inability to provoke the Nandi to pitched battle. Yet within a few months, the Nandi had risen again. Thefts of railway material resumed, a Boer trader and a missionary were killed, stock was stolen from Boer settlers, murders continued along the railway and even the sub-station at Soba was attacked. Indeed, by 1905, notwithstanding the expeditions recorded here and various other police actions, it seemed as if the British were further from conquering Nandi than they had been at the start of the conflict.

The resilience of the Nandi resistance may be attributed to a secret they shared with their enemy and which had propelled the British to world dominance. This was the adoption of the ancient Roman attitude to combat, which held that once a nation had set its face to war, it had to fight on until the last enemy had been humbled or until it had no more men of fighting age left alive. Other adversaries of the British might submit before being reduced to such a state of prostration, but the Nandi would no more consider such dishonour than would have the British themselves.

Such humiliation at the hands of "natives" could not be tolerated and the British had to come up with a solution to preserve the prestige of their Empire. It was at this point that a new actor entered the stage, one possessing a ruthlessness and guile that would turn the course of Nandi history.

Chapter 5

A messenger from Hell

On 12th May 1902, the German ship, *Safari,* pulled into the Mombasa harbour. One passenger, a British lieutenant arriving in Africa for the first time, wrote in his diary:

"The spick and span town, the vivid green and freshness of the country, the palm trees and the old Arab buildings, formed a picture which was not only quite new to me but of extreme natural beauty."

The sight cheered the diarist after a voyage he had found miserable. He had made no friends and alienated the numerous German officers on board when he had interrupted their torture of a monkey and informed them that they were cowardly savages. He did not mention in his diary entry his own German ancestry, in fact, throughout his life, he would pretend to be of Danish descent.

That he was able to get away with this story is a little surprising since his German grandfather, the banker Daniel Meinertzhagen, had been naturalised by a special Act of Parliament and his family were, alongside the Rothschild's, one of the two most prominent Anglo-German families in England, possessing over the Rothschild's the advantage of not being Jewish. Yet throughout his life, Richard Meinertzhagen, our diarist, would possess the ability to reshape his history after his own imagination.

His physical presence was of a piece with the legend he would become. Tall and broad, with penetrating hazel brown eyes set in a long angular face, Meinertzhagen cast a large shadow, both literally and figuratively. At the time of our story, he did not yet sport the glasses he wore in later life. He did, however, wear the moustache that was compulsory for all British soldiers until 1916 and which he retained even after leaving the army. Some photos show him wearing a beard.

His deeds, meanwhile, were even more impressive than his physique. He played a pivotal role in Britain's intelligence services over several decades. He engineered a crucial British victory against the Turks in the First World War. He met Hitler in Berlin to plead the cause of Germany's Jews, ever after cursing himself for not using the loaded revolver he had carried in his pocket. At the age of 70, he took part in a firefight with Arab snipers and saved a group of Israeli soldiers. He was a brilliant ornithologist who discovered numerous sub-species of birds and generously donated his huge stuffed bird collection to the British Museum.

This was the account of himself which he told and which was almost universally accepted in his lifetime. The first and last claims alone had a grain of truth. He played a small but significant part in British intelligence in the First World War and did donate a large bird collection to the British Museum. Yet as Brian Garfield has shown in *The Meinertzhagen Mystery*, many of the birds were stolen from the same museum in the first place and many of the new sub-species turned out to be confected from two birds stitched together. As for the other claims, they were all invented from whole cloth, along with numerous other lies that Meinertzhagen told.

Garfield has demonstrated that many parts of his published diaries were written after the event so we cannot even be sure whether the story of the monkey-baiting Germans was invented. Nor can we uncritically swallow Meinertzhagen's compelling descriptions of various other incidents that allegedly occurred during his first tour of Kenya. These tales include his command to his men to shoot a troop of baboons after a baboon had killed his dog and his order to exterminate an entire village responsible for killing a white man, excepting only children. Various other slaughters are also recorded. Yet we need not assume that Meinertzhagen lied about everything. So, though Garfield is inclined to believe that many of his reports of massacres were invented, Nandi oral testimony suggests that if he lied about his crimes it was to play them down rather than to exaggerate them. In addition, there is ample testimony to his physical courage; in the words of one friend he was "as indifferent to physical pain as to personal danger." He was a bully but not a coward.

He was certainly a reactionary, however, fanatically opposed to new movements such as socialism and the campaign for votes for women. This despite, or perhaps because of the fact, that he was related to many of the leading progressive intellectuals of his day. Thus, for example, his aunt Beatrice Webb would co-author with her husband the constitution of the British Labour Party. In his diaries, he describes telling an admirer of his Aunt how much damage he believed she was doing.

Nevertheless, Meinertzhagen was capable of expressing more enlightened sentiments. *The Kenya Diary,* Meinertzhagen's book, represents him opining that Kenya should be a black man's country and that the encouragement of white settlement was a mistake. In addition, he writes with some passion about the mistreatment of the Nandi by civilian officer Walter Mayes.

Mayes, according to Meinertzhagen, was a man of the lowest possible character who had washed up in Africa as a distressed British seaman. The shortage of whites in Africa had led the government to employ him. He had previously married a non-white woman, a Mauritian Creole, whom he had abandoned but who followed him to Africa, forcing him to throw out his Nandi concubines. He was a drunk and a thief and his brutal treatment of the local people contributed to the unrest in Nandi. The bulk of the cattle he stole from the local people he kept for himself rather than turning them over to the government.

One important fact to bear in mind when weighing these assessments is that it was Mayes who would challenge Meinertzhagen's account of the death of Koitaleel and provoke his fury. Meinertzhagen would ensure that Mayes was branded a liar. Mayes was ruined socially, or he would have been had he had any social status to begin with. His apparently humble origins and his marriage to a non-white woman ensured that he had little to lose. He settled down amongst the Nandi and "went native".

It may seem odd that the Nandi would embrace one who had oppressed them so harshly, but the community does not remember him as an exploiter. Rather, he is recalled as a generous and honourable man who stood as a friend to the people in their hour of need. His wife also inspired affection and her grave was lovingly tended long after her death. It is Meinertzhagen whose name stinks in their nostrils as the murderer of their leader and the destroyer of their nation. Meinertzhagen's contemporary, Sigmund Freud, would have had no hesitation in diagnosing the workings of denial and projection in the diary entries that accuse Mayes of the very brutality which the diarist himself was guilty of.

Official sources also paint a picture of Mayes that contrasts with Meinertzhagen's. He was variously described by those who promoted him as "a plucky little man, who got on exceedingly well with all Africans" and "a well educated man, very good at accounts, and speaking the native languages with fluency."

The accusations against Mayes appear in the diary accounts of both Meinertzhagen's first and second tours of duty in Kenya, though only part of his first sojourn was spent in Nandi. It was during the second tour that he took on the task that so many before him had failed to accomplish, to dispose of the threat to the Empire represented by the Nandi Oorgoiyoot who the British referred to as the Laibon.

He began his task by setting up an intelligence service, recruiting the Maasai to spy on the Nandi and to seek the whereabouts of Koitaleel. The usefulness of this service may be cast in doubt by Meinertzhagen's repeated description of Koitaleel as an old man. He does say at one point that Koitaleel was "about 40" but one may wonder if this was added later. It would seem odd to describe a man of forty, or even 45 – Koitaleel's actual age – as old. It seems likely that Meinertzhagen simply assumed that an African leader would be an old man.

More accurate was Meinertzhagen's claim that "the Laibon" was constantly agitating against the British and that the Nandi elders met frequently to discuss how to drive the British out. In the same diary entry, he wrote that murders and raids were being reported from every part of the district.

Absurdly, he attributed this culmination of a ten-year struggle for freedom to the alleged misdeeds of Walter Mayes. It seems that

Meinertzhagen was unable to imagine that the Nandi might view the invasion of their homeland in exactly the same way that he would have viewed an invasion of his.

The Nandi did not confine themselves to seeking to resist British incursions into their lands. They continued to raid both inside and outside their heartlands, with the few white settlers serving as the primary target. As Charles Miller describes in *The Lunatic Express*, the Nandi stole their cattle "with almost clockwork regularity" and even scouted the perimeter of Lord Delamere's Equator ranch, more than 40 miles from the disturbed area. Another stockman saw three of his workers fall to Nandi spears in broad daylight just a short distance from his veranda.

On another occasion, a British District Officer is said to have sent a clerk to a Nandi village demanding that they pay the hut tax. The clerk's head was returned in a sack. "Here is the hut tax of the Nandi!" was the message.

Meinertzhagen reports in his diary that one of his men, who had taken leave to go and purchase a wife, was murdered by the Nandi and his rifle and ammunition stolen. Immediately after this incident, Meinertzhagen says his company encountered around 300 Nandi spearmen. He gave then ten minutes to disperse. They complied but tried to set an ambush further along the path, which was discovered by the advance guard. Again they were ordered to disperse. They left shouting threats. A conference of Nandi "chiefs" was called to discuss the murder of the soldier and the rising unrest. Koitaleel wisely refused to attend. The British warned that the Nandi living near the railway would be forced to move if trouble continued.

Another ambush of Meinertzhagen was attempted, according to his diary, by about thirty warriors, one of whom was killed and another wounded and captured. Thereafter, Meinertzhagen's house was pelted with stones and arrows three nights in a row. On 12th August 1905, he wrote that he had captured the culprits, five boys and a girl whom he locked in the guard room before spanking the boys and setting both them and the girl to work in his garden.

The next day, the British issued the Nandi with an ultimatum. For their misdeeds they were to pay a fine of 300 head of cattle within three weeks. Refusal would be met with a military expedition. Meinertzhagen predicted that the Nandi would roar with laughter at the proposal.

Plans for the expedition were put in hand on the assumption (which proved correct) that the Nandi would continue to defy the British. The focus of activity was Fort Kaptumo ("Nandi Fort"), which by this time had replaced Kipture as the administrative centre. The increasing concentration of British troops led to a diminution in the number of Nandi attacks but failed to frighten the people into submission. Meinertzhagen began teaching the porters attached to his company how to shoot in preparation for the expedition.

On the 26th of September, Meinertzhagen wrote that Koitaleel had convened a large representative meeting of the whole Nandi community, at which it was decided that the British government was afraid of the Nandi, that no expedition would materialise and that, therefore, the Nandi should escalate their aggressive tactics and drive all government officials from the district.

He claims that the meeting also resolved to have him murdered. He continues,

"The situation now resolves itself into a personal quarrel between me and the Laibon and I will bet a small sum that he falls first."

This is one of several occasions in which Meinertzhagen claims to know the secrets of Koitaleel's councils. Some of the intentions he attributes to the Oorgoiyoot contradict Nandi sources but it is not only for that reason that we should be sceptical. His intelligence was obtained, he says, using agents drawn from the local colony of Uasin Nkishu Maasai. He wrote that they hated the Nandi but could move amongst them freely. He claims to have Maasai agents living "in some capacity" with Koitaleel and other Nandi leaders.

In writing this, Meinertzhagen may have imagined that Nandi chiefs were like English gentlemen, waited on by a large domestic staff into which a spy might perhaps be slipped as a groom or footman. In reality, any who attended to Koitaleel would surely have been trusted intimates and not hirelings drawn from a colony of collaborators.

Meinertzhagen does not even pretend to have had any significant Nandi agents. There were a few Nandi prepared to "eat their own feet", in Koitaleel's phrase, some hundreds even fought with the British against their own people, but there was only one with access to Koitaleel who might have betrayed him to Meinertzhagen. That was Meinertzhagen's interpreter, Letangwo, who had limited access to the Oorgoiyoot. Yet Meinertzhagen does not quote him as the source of his information and instead accuses Letangwo of plotting against him with Koitaleel.

It may be noted here that the fact that the Nandi living near the British were willing to trade with them does not necessarily mean that they should be regarded as collaborators. In most cases, cooperation was of a limited sort and did not extend to serving as porters to the British. In similar fashion, Nandi "chiefs" would listen to lectures from British officials and then proceed to ignore them. There were amongst the Nandi some who might be described as traitors, above all those who fought with the British, but the bulk of the Nandi fully supported the common struggle.

Nevertheless, Meinertzhagen did have Nandi friends. Indeed, one elderly Nandi entrusted Meinertzhagen with the care of his three daughters, anticipating the coming campaign and fearing that they would otherwise have to hide in the forest. The presence of these pubescent girls led some to suspect Meinertzhagen of dishonourable intentions. It is unlikely that these critics would have been assuaged by reading Meinertzhagen's boast of getting the girls to pose for guests as Nandi warriors, painted white and red, but otherwise stark naked.

It is rather unlikely, however, that Nandi collaborators like the father of these girls would have been in a position to provide much useful intelligence about the Oorgoiyoot. Moreover, whatever the quality of Meinertzhagen's intelligence, he failed entirely to understand the position of Koitaleel, describing him as a dictator. It seems he could not understand that the Oorgoiyoot led his people not by threats of violence but by spiritual influence. The Nandi followed Koitaleel because he was the anointed of Assiis and because he had inspired them to deeds that had formerly seemed impossible.

Meinertzhagen's description of a dictatorial Koitaleel may just reflect his ignorance or it may be a deliberate attempt to besmirch his name. His claims about Koitaleel's intentions, meanwhile, are clearly intended to justify the murder of the Oorgoiyoot. Thus, his diary entry for the 28th of September represents Koitaleel as plotting to ambush him in order to obtain his body parts for magical purposes. He goes on to affirm the need to kill or capture Koitaleel arguing that his death might make the planned punitive expedition unnecessary.

The expedition that Meinertzhagen hoped to avoid was taking shape as he wrote. It consisted of 1,320 men from the King's African Rifles, 260 armed police, 1,000 Maasai levies, 100 Somali levies, 500 armed porters and 3,460 unarmed porters. In addition, there were 80 British officers and numerous medical, veterinary and other non-combatant personnel. The force had 10 machine guns and two armoured railway carriages. Thus, there were 3,260 armed men. One may consider here that according to Bill Ruto's prologue to the second volume of Matson's *Nandi Resistance to British Rule*, the number of active Nandi warriors may have been reduced to as few as 2,000 before this time. Matson himself, meanwhile, puts the number of potential warriors at 6,000, including uninitiated youths and junior elders. That the British should field an expedition similar in size to the potential opposition was remarkable in the context of "native" wars. As noted, in such wars, numbers were traditionally regarded as largely irrelevant, technical superiority being sufficient to guarantee victory. The spirit of the Nandi and the genius of the Oorgoiyoot had forced the British to recalculate and this time they intended to take no chances.

Meanwhile, Meinertzhagen had received permission from his superiors to kill or capture Koitaleel. In the same diary entry that he records this, he also claims that an assassination attempt was made on him by an agent of the Oorgoiyoot. A beautiful young girl was sent to poison him but was frustrated by Meinertzhagen's discovery of the poison. He says he sent her back to Koitaleel with a recommendation that the Oorgoiyoot take the poison himself.

In his next diary entry, he announces that he has received a plan of Koitaleel's village, which consisted, he says, of twenty huts, with the "Laibon" sleeping in a different one each night. This perhaps is the sort of information that his agents could have obtained and we know that the British had previously received information on the Oorgoiyoot's whereabouts that brought them close to capturing him. Meinertzhagen here repeats his claim that Koitaleel plans to invite him to talks and ambush him.

On 18th October 1905, he writes that he has arranged for a meeting with Koitaleel on the following day and states that the interpreter who arranged the meeting was heard by Meinertzhagen's agents plotting with the Oorgoiyoot. His entry concludes melodramatically,

"Come what will, I will meet him tomorrow and during the next 24 hours I suspect that either he or I will have said goodbye to this world; I do not really very much care which of us it is."

Chapter 6

The sun goes down

Now Koitaleel did not love war. He could not consent to the surrender of his people's land or liberties but he knew that talk of freedom did not fill bellies and when he heard the cries of hungry infants and the mourning of those whose loved ones had fallen in the struggle, his heart yearned for peace. He had already consented to several truces to allow his people to recover from the ravages imposed by the series of British expeditions and police actions. He would even have been willing to let the British have their railway had it not been for his certainty that the completion of that work heralded the end of the Nandi nation. As it was, though a loyal son of his father, he had strained every sinew to delay the fulfilment of Kimnyolei's prophecy of the iron snake. Since the railway had already been inaugurated, then Koitaleel's best hope was to seek to put off the accomplishment of the unfulfilled clauses of his father's prophecy in the way that he had delayed the completion of the railway.

We do not suggest that he thought he could undo the curse that had been sealed in blood. Nevertheless, pessimism of the intellect can be joined to optimism of the will and while Koitaleel knew that the story of the Nandi nation must come to an end, he yet hoped to insert another chapter before the last. He would willingly have consented to another truce, to leaving the railway alone in return for the British leaving the Nandi in possession of their heartland and free to follow the customs and laws of their ancestors. He did not deceive himself that this was likely, Kimnyolei had promised him "a time and a season" and to have lived for ten years after assuming the throne was more than he had expected, but it was his duty to keep hope alive, and he pleaded with Assiis for a stay of execution, if not for himself then at least for his people.

When he received the proposal for a meeting with Meinertzhagen for peace negotiations, his heart leapt even as his inner voice told him that that day would be his last. His advisers warned him with one voice that the offer was a trap, and Koitaleel did not argue with them. He simply insisted that he would go nonetheless. He was willing to stake his life even upon the slimmest chance of relieving his people's suffering. He knew that another Nandi campaign was in the offing and that the British had collected together a greater force than ever before and feared that this expedition would prove to be a mortal blow to the Nandi nation. If there was any possibility that it could be averted by a promise to leave the railway alone, it was an opportunity that he had to grasp.

Thus, while Koitaleel anticipated his death at the hands of the white man, he knew that even the ancestors see the future through a veil but dimly, and it was the hope of peace, however faint, that acquitted him of suicide and justified his walking into a probable trap. He also surely hoped that in the much more likely event that he was murdered, his sacrifice would not be in vain. He made arrangements to ensure that the Nandi would continue to fight on after his death and he may have speculated that such a continuation of the struggle would persuade the British to accept that the root of the Nandi's stubbornness lay not in the influence of a single man but in the people's common passion for liberty. In such an event, the intent to incorporate Nandi into the Empire might have been abandoned and a lasting peace agreed between the British and the Nandi. Then too he may have speculated that by handing the British the appearance of a victory at the start of the campaign, he could thereby mitigate its severity. Having salvaged their pride by destroying their foremost enemy, maybe the British would be content with fewer Nandi corpses and fewer burnt villages and food stores. We cannot know exactly how Koitaleel thought his death might benefit his people, but we do know that he believed it to be his duty to them to meet with Meinertzhagen, even if it meant his own end. However, he also had a duty to his family and, anticipating the likelihood of his death, he imitated his father and sent his children to safety.

It had been agreed between the Oorgoiyoot and Meinertzhagen that each man should be accompanied by just five companions. Koitaleel chose his five closest companions: Kipitguut araap Chemurungu, Cheliilim, araap Chelogis, araap Mosoonik and Sato. In addition to the five selected, he took 18 bodyguards. No violation of the agreement was intended, Koitaleel always meant to meet Meinertzhagen with the permitted party of five and to separate from the guards once the meeting place was reached. The bringing of bodyguards was intended simply as a precaution against British violation of the agreement. Five men armed with spears would be no match for five with rifles; another 18 might be a deterrent.

Meinertzhagen was to use the fact that Koitaleel brought bodyguards, as well as the fiction that he had additional men concealed in the bush, to justify his claim that the Oorgoiyoot had been planning an ambush. Yet Meinertzhagen himself brought 80 men of the King's African Rifles, as well as a Maxim gun.

The King's African Rifles was a regiment composed of men from various warrior races who had discovered that there was no less pleasure to be had from killing for the British than had formerly been obtained from disposing of the enemies of their traditional rulers. Meinertzhagen's diary entries are testimony to the fierce character of these men. Thus, for example, his entry from June 1903 describes how a mock battle between Maasai and Sudanese soldiers got out of hand to the extent of causing three deaths.

He also recounts a story about a corporal from the Manyema people, whose custom it was to eat their enemies in order to absorb their strength. Meinertzhagen says he found the corporal with five black hands stuck in his belt. On being questioned the corporal explained this was his supper, the fingers being the tenderest parts of a man, though not as tender as the buttocks of a young girl.

This man may perhaps be identified with Corporal Simba Manyema (one of the five men selected by Meinertzhagen to accompany him to the meeting with Koitaleel), on the assumption that he took the name of his people as a surname.

Since Meinertzhagen was a compulsive liar, we do not know if these stories are true. However, it is significant that these were the kind of stories that were readily believed about the King's African Rifles. Moreover, whether or not any soldiers of the K.A.R. ever practiced cannibalism, the Nandi and other peoples who faced them bear witness that the men of this regiment were merciless enemies.

These then were the type of men who formed the column of 80 riflemen that set out from "Nandi Fort" (Kaptumo) at 5.00 am on 19th

October 1905. The temperature would have been cool; the sun would not yet have risen. It would have taken a while for the marching men to work up a sweat, though the going would have been tougher for the men struggling with the Maxim gun. The terrain between Nandi Fort and the appointed meeting place at Keet Parak Hill was challenging, a straight path would have required crossing ridges, steep hills and valleys. Given these difficulties and the absence of bridges, it is likely that Meinertzhagen took an indirect route to avoid crossing rivers. Except the Mokong River, the local streams and rivers have their source in the Nandi Hills. Thus, one can avoid crossing them by going upstream.

We think that the party would have gone North for almost half the distance to Mugundoi Village before turning eastward to avoid the Kaitit Tributary of the Kundos River. Passing on to the western ridge of Kosoiywo Hill, they would have followed the line of the valley looking for the stretch of drier land through the swamp that forms the source of one of the tributaries of the Mosombor River. As they emerged from the swampy ridge and the canopy of trees entangled with the climber, **Sinendeet**, the men would have had their first glimpse of the summit of Keet Parak Hill. This itinerary is consistent with Meinertzhagen's statement that his journey to Keet Parak and back covered 24 miles.

The trek to the meeting place would not have been regarded as a hardship by the tough men of the K.A.R and the hypnotic rhythm of the march and perhaps the singing of songs would have made the time appear to pass more quickly. At Keet Parak, Meinertzhagen would have surveyed the area to check that the Nandi had not observed his arrival. The appointed meeting place was directly behind the hill on the eastern side.

According to Meinertzhagen's report to his superiors, the column arrived at Keet Parak Hill at 8.47 a.m. Meinertzhagen hid the bulk of his men in a hollow, where they would be hidden from the view of the Nandi. Perhaps equally important, though Meinertzhagen does not say so, this arrangement ensured that the 75 men he thus concealed would be unable to witness what passed at the meeting. Lieutenant Butler, the other white officer, mounted the machine gun to cover the meeting place. Meinertzhagen selected native officer Mbaruk Effendi, Corporal Simba Manyema and three others to accompany him. At 10.30am, the Oorgoiyoot approached the meeting place with his counsellors and bodyguards. Thus far, the British and Nandi accounts are in agreement.

Meinertzhagen stated that the Oorgoiyoot arrived with 22 warriors in a breach of the agreed arrangements. He also said that Koitaleel had many more warriors concealed nearby. He wrote that his Maasai agents informed him that the trap to catch him was complete and that the Laibon (Koitaleel) had some 300 spearmen secreted in the bush near the meeting place. He claimed further that on advancing into full view of the Laibon, it was clear that he had some 50 armed men about him.

The Nandi recollection is that there was a woman, Cheepo Rorio, watching from a distance, and perhaps some other spectators, women and children, standing yet further away hoping for a distant glimpse of the white man. The claim that there were 300 concealed warriors and that Koitaleel was accompanied by a party of 50 seems to be simply Meinertzhagen's fiction. Koitaleel brought his party of five and the 18 bodyguards, making a total of 23 followers. He approached the meeting place with grass in his hand, a sign of peace. Deciding what happened next is difficult as both Meinertzhagen's diary and the Nandi oral sources offer two distinct accounts. One version from each side claims that Meinertzhagen and Koitaleel shook hands, the other from each state that they did not.

In the first of Meinertzhagen's diary accounts, allegedly written shortly after his return to Nandi Fort, he states:

"I advanced to meet the Laibon with five men. As I suspected, he ambushed me as soon as I shook hands with him; but we were ready and he, the interpreter and several others, some 23 in all, were left dead."

His alternative account, which reproduces his official report to Colonel Harrison, filed the next day, states that Koitaleel refused to shake hands. He writes:

"I halted my small party within four paces of the Laibon and asked him to come forward and shake hands. He replied that the sun was too hot, which, of course was a ridiculous statement from a native. I also considered it wrong that a white man should have to make advances to a native, so I replied, "Very well, we will conduct our conversation at this distance. Shall we sit down?"

No sooner was this interpreted than the Laibon made a quick sign and an arrow pierced the sleeve of my shirt. The interpreter wheeled round on me, making as if to strike me with his spear but was instantly shot by my corporal. I seized the Laibon and dragged him forward, getting scratched by his spear and an arrow knocked off my helmet. The Laibon wrenched himself free, but by dragging him towards me I had prevented having spears thrown at me, as they would most certainly have hit him. Both I and my party at once opened fire. I am unable to state with certainty what followed. The Laibon was shot simultaneously by myself and my native officer, and several dead were left at the meeting place including several of the Laibon's near relations. I took two stone headed knobkerries from the Laibon's belt."

Against this we have the two Nandi accounts, one of which says Meinertzhagen shot Koitaleel after the Oorgoiyoot refused to shake hands; the other that he was shot at point black range after a brief handshake. Both accounts agree that there was no attempt to ambush Meinertzhagen. Both versions also agree in ascribing a malevolent role to the interpreter Letongwo. In the first, the interpreter told Koitaleel not to shake the white man's hand as his skin would stick to the Oorgoiyoot's palm while telling Meinertzhagen that a refusal to shake would be the signal for an ambush. In the second, he advised that any handshake be kept brief for the same reason while telling Meinertzhagen that a brief handshake would signal an ambush.

The Nandi remembrance would seem to be too kind to Meinertzhagen. It suggests that he may have killed the Oorgoiyoot on the spur of the moment, believing that he was about to be attacked. Had this been the case, it would have made sense for him to have kept the interpreter alive as a witness to his good faith and the treachery of the Oorgoiyoot. Instead, Letongwo was shot along with Koitaleel. We can assume that Meinertzhagen wanted to kill all witnesses to his crime who were not complicit in it. Yet this assumption only makes sense if it is accepted that he knew that he was committing a crime. Here we may note that he himself admits that he went to Keet Parak Hill with the intention of killing Koitaleel. He justifies this by saying that he received intelligence warning of an ambush but he says that this information came from spies, rather than from Letongwo, and that these same spies implicated the interpreter in Koitaleels's perfidy. Moreover, he also admits that he had considered doing away with Letongwo even before the day of the meeting with the Oorgoiyoot.

Assuming that Letongwo did tell Koitaleel not to shake hands, or to keep his handshake brief, we cannot be sure that he did so in bad faith. He might have told the Oorgoiyoot not to shake hands because he suspected Meinertzhagen of planning to kill Koitaleel when he came forward. Meanwhile, the suggestion that he was feeding Meinertzhagen's fears of an ambush is pure speculation. We cannot know if Letongwo hoped for Koitaleel's death; we do know that if he was on Meinertzhagen's side, Meinertzhagen rewarded him with a bullet. Indeed, we cannot even rule out the possibility that, enraged by the murder of the Oorgoiyoot, he turned his spear on Meinertzhagen as Meinertzhagen claimed in the report to Colonel Harrison. Nevertheless, the Nandi have remembered Letongwo as a traitor.

The one thing that all four accounts agree on is that Meinertzhagen shot Koitaleel. Yet even this is open to doubt. In addition to the two versions of his story in his *Kenya Diary*, Meinertzhagen left behind another in the form of a heliograph relay message to his superior Pope-Hennessy sent hours after the Oorgoiyoot's murder, which was preserved in the official records. This reads:

"As soon as I came in full view of him (Koitaleel) I realised that he was assembled with 12 warriors around him and about 20 behind the bush and at once his intent dawned on me, but considering the advantage his death would be to the forthcoming operation I proceeded with my five men. Just before I was about to shake hands with him, my interpreter, who is the Laibon's spy, wheeled round and was about to spear one of my men when I shot him dead; spears and arrows flew at a range of only four yards, but the only ones which hit were one arrow in my helmet and one spear through my sleeve. I at once seized the Laibon who was promptly shot by Mbaruk Effendi. Several of his followers fell to our rifles and the remainder fled. The enemy had 23 killed, our casualties were nil. I trust my actions meet with your approval."

Thus, following the earliest of Meinertzhagen's reports to his superiors, Mbaruk Effendi alone killed Koitaleel. As a general rule, one would be inclined to give priority to the earlier account. It is not clear if this rule applies here. For example, in the heliograph message, he puts the number of the Oorgoiyoot's followers at 12, but the figure of 22 given in the official report tallies better with the Nandi figure of 23. More importantly, the message to Pope-Hennessy makes no mention of the Maxim gun while while the official report does, though it skilfully obscures the question as to whether the gun was put to use.

In an unpublished typescript of his *Kenya Diary,* Meinertzhagen was more forthcoming on this point. He wrote:

"Before going down to meet the Laibon I had warned Butler to open fire at once if he saw us being overwhelmed. He mounted the machine gun and covered the place of meeting. An arrow knocked off my helmet and Butler, thinking I was down and seeing the hand to hand fighting going on opened fire. The bullets flew thick among us and I don't know how we escaped. One bullet just grazed my shin, which has done no more than give me a stiff leg and one of my men Jumia Wad Malhi was hit in the fleshy part of the neck."

As Brian Garfield notes, we have no idea when this unpublished excerpt was written. Even if it formed part of the original diary entry for 19th October, it would still postdate the message to Pope-Hennessy, which can presumably be identified with the "brief wire to Headquarters" referred to in that entry. Nevertheless, it tends to reinforce the supposition that his first report to his superiors was in some respects less honest than the second. Presumably, on reflection, he decided that he could not get away with cutting out the role of the Maxim altogether.

This leaves the question as to which, if either, of the two reports should be believed when considering who shot Koitaleel; the first in which Mbaruk shoots the Oorgoiyoot and Meinertzhagen kills the interpreter, or the second in which Mbaruk and Meinertzhagen shoot Koitaleel "simultaneously" while Corporal Simba disposes of the treacherous interpreter. In favour of the earlier report, here is the consideration that Meinertzhagen often stole the credit due to others but rarely shared or gave away that which he believed due to himself. So we have a reason why he might have falsely claimed to have shot Koitaleel but no clear reason for him to falsely deny having done so.

Brian Garfield, however, suggests the possibility that it was neither Meinertzhagen nor Mbaruk Effendi who killed the Oorgoiyoot. He reasons:

"What really happened at Ket Parak Hill was simple and stark. Richard Meinertzhagen (RM) posted Lieutenant Butler with a half company of men in hiding above the appointed meeting place. RM took his five-man escort down to the meeting. Sammy Butler was an excellent shot with his new Maxim machine gun.

The lie of the land at Ket Parak Hill; the placement of the trees and the distance to the hollow, shows that the machine gun must have been set up 75 yards from the site where the warriors died. Machine guns are not precision weapons. The Maxim gun had an effective range much greater than 75 yards, but the gun could not be relied upon for pinpoint accuracy. It would lay down a pattern of fire – a lot of bullets in a very short time (eight per second). In terms of inflicting damage, it would be deadliest when fired into a tight group of people. It could easily kill them all in a few seconds. But some bullets inevitably would miss the targets, perhaps go wide or perhaps ricochet off in unintended directions. Therefore, RM and his five men must have been some distance short of their meeting with the Nandi. Otherwise RM's party would have been at risk from being hit by stray bullets.

That's why it is likely that RM did not actually shoot anyone that day. He carried only a sidearm, and most likely was too far away for effective shooting."

The problem with this theory is that it contradicts not only Meinertzhagen's accounts but also those of the Nandi who have no reason to lie. Moreover, the assumption that Meinertzhagen would have followed the safest course contradicts Garfield's own portrait of a man addicted to insane risks. The odds must, therefore, be that the Oorgoiyoot was shot either by Meinertzhagen or Mbaruk Effendi or by both. However, it needs to be explained why Meinertzhagen didn't do as Garfield proposes. Given that he could have had the Nandi mown down without putting his person in danger, why did he put himself at risk from Nandi spears and British bullets?

A possible answer is that Meinertzhagen needed to know that Koitaleel was present. Never before had the Oorgoiyoot agreed to meet the British and he might have relented and sent a substitute. It would have been a disaster for Meinertzhagen to have ordered the massacre only to discover that Koitaleel was not amongst the dead. He may have remembered here that the British had previously claimed to have killed Koitaleel only to find out that rumours of the Oorgoiyoot's death had been greatly exaggerated. So he needed Koitaleel to come forward and identify himself, which required that Meinertzhagen himself come forward.

If we reject Garfield's theory, we are brought back to the question as to whether Koitaleel was shot by Mbaruk alone or by both Mbaruk and Meinertzhagen. We might assume that Mbaruk had been ordered to shoot the Oorgoiyoot while the attention of Koitaleel and his followers was focused on Meinertzhagen since this would make tactical sense. Meinertzhagen's other four men must also have been prepared and thus each man would probably have marked one of Koitaleel's counsellors. Meinertzhagen's second report stated that his five chosen men "approached with rifles at full cock and loaded, also with bayonets fixed." If Mbaruk shot Koitaleel and each of the other men shot one of Koitaleel's counsellors, that would have left one of the Oorgoiyoot's men alive after the first volley, unless he was killed by Meinertzhagen. However, even if Meinertzhagen shot one of the counsellors, he could still have put a bullet into Koitaleel thereafter, and there remains the possibility that both Meinertzhagen and Mbaruk did indeed fire on the Oorgoiyoot simultaneously. Presumably, Butler opened fire on the bodyguards with the Maxim as soon as shooting began. Even with the distance between the Oorgoiyoot and his counsellors on the one hand and the bodyguards behind them on the other, there would have been a risk of stray bullets hitting the British party. Yet the alternative of waiting till Meinertzhagen and his men had ducked back would have put them in danger of Nandi spears.

The Nandi account holds that Koitaleel staggered for almost a hundred metres before collapsing by a Simatweet tree. If so, it could be that Meinertzhagen might have put a bullet into the wounded Oorgoiyoot from a distance after ducking back out of the way of the Maxim bullets. Still, Nandi oral history affirms that Koitaleel was shot by Meinertzhagen after shaking hands or else as he was about to shake. Perhaps Cheepo Rorio, the Nandi woman witness who is the source for the Nandi account, couldn't see who shot the Oorgoiyoot and simply assumed that it was Meinertzhagen. Or perhaps, Meinertzhagen's second report is right and both he and Mbaruk shot Koitaleel at the same time. Meanwhile, even if Meinertzhagen never shot Koitaleel and instead deputed Mbaruk to do the job, he would have been no less the Oorgoiyoot's murderer. Brian Garfield, in correspondence with the authors, agrees that some of the Nandi may have been felled with rifles and that Koitaleel may have been shot by one of Meinertzhagen's companions at close range. Meinertzhagen himself, he points out, would have been trying to look innocent and thus would not have had a gun in his hand.

It is certainly believable that Meinertzhagen would have wanted to be the one, or at least one of the two, who shot Koitaleel. He was a patriot and a narcissist; he may have wanted not only to claim the credit for ridding the British Empire of this turbulent priest king, but to actually deserve it. He was also a big game hunter who may have wanted the satisfaction of adding the Oorgoiyoot's head to his bag.

This may be more than a figure of speech. When the Nandi returned to the site of the massacre, they found that Koitaleel's head was missing. Many, therefore, believe that the British decapitated Koitaleel and kept his head in order that they could examine it in the hope of understanding the Oorgoiyoot's military prowess. A psychoanalytic interpretation of Meinertzhagen's diary might place weight on his statement that: "…the death of the Laibon has completely knocked the stuffing out of the Nandi and has left them without a head." Nevertheless, he does not say that he left the body of Koitaleel in the same state even though it was the kind of thing he might have boasted about.

One Nandi tradition holds that the removal of the Oorgoiyoot's head was revenge for the beheading of the white man whose skull had been demanded by Koitaleel. The reader will recall that the flesh from the white man's head was eaten by the two hungry Nandi sharpshooters. The evidence we have cited from Meinertzhagen's diary, suggesting that Corporal Simba may have been a cannibal opens up the theoretical possibility that Koitaleel's head may have met the same fate. Meinertzhagen gives a desire to absorb the strength of the enemy as the chief explanation of Manyema cannibalism and the eating of the Oorgoiyoot's flesh would make sense in this context, assuming that Meinertzhagen for whatever reason, allowed Corporal Simba to carry away the head. A report appeared in the Kenyan press suggesting that the head might be held in the Pitt Rivers Museum in Oxford. In response to our own investigation, the Pitt Rivers Museum has strongly

81

denied this accusation. The British Museum and The Natural History Museum, both of which had connections to Meinertzhagen, have also denied possessing the head, as has the Imperial War Museum. An unsourced story reported by the Kumekucha website claims that the skull is now in the hands of a Japanese collector and that the hole in the skull is more consistent with a shot from a rifle than a sidearm. Unless definitive evidence emerges, however, the ultimate end of Koitaleel's head will remain a mystery.

Turning to the question of the number of people who were killed at Keet Parak Hill, Meinertzhagen consistently held to the figure of 23, the Nandi count comes to 25 including the interpreter. We may assume Meinertzhagen sincerely believed his figure; it would have made little sense to knock just two off the real total. It is unlikely the British would have stopped to count the dead so Meinertzhagen must have depended on a headcount or estimate made prior to the action and may have miscounted or misremembered. Alternatively, the Nandi recollection of the number of bodyguards may overstate the true figure by two.

Where Meinertzhagen's account deliberately misleads is in suggesting that some of Koitaleel's warriors survived. Cheepo Rorio, the woman witness who saw the action from a distance was able to escape, but Koitaleel's party were wiped out to the last man. We can assume that Meinertzhagen didn't want to leave any witnesses not complicit in his crime and that he would have killed Cheepo Rorio if he could have.

His accounts of the return journey home are also masterpieces of misdirection, stating that he had to engage parties of the enemy on the way back to Nandi Fort. It is true that the returning soldiers were chased by Nandi warriors. It is also true that the route back home was treated as a "free fire zone". Any Nandi within range were shot, without any attempt being made to determine if they were a threat or any effort to distinguish by sex or age. The British left Keet Parak by the southerly route, opposite to the way they had arrived. At the next village, they came across men and women who had just finished harvesting millet. It was a custom amongst the Nandi that people from different homesteads would come together and harvest as a team. After the harvest had been gathered they would celebrate with a specially made beer known as *Maiyekaap Mosore*. The British soldiers bayoneted the villagers and smashed their faces. This village was subsequently named *Keteng* after *Koteny* meaning "dead". Within this village are *Kipekelek* and *Chemunuun* meaning "toothless men and women", commemorating the shattering of the victims' jaws. After the company crossed the river, hotly pursued by enraged Nandi warriors, they massacred a large party of boys (recent initiates). This site is called **Kaarbataarus** (initiates killed). On encountering a young girl, Chesasa Cheepo Torotwo, with her child, they killed both on the spot before wading into the reedy swamp, from which they could see Nandi Fort protruding beyond Mosombor Ridge. At Kaapsoo, a group of herdboys tried to hide as they saw the British soldiers advancing towards them. One of the boys, araap Yakong, hiding in a tree, was shot in the testicle but survived and was rescued by Nandi warriors. He lived to old age, though childless. According to the late Simion araap Mugun, in 1950, araap Yakong mounted a non-violent protest against British rule by exposing his wound in the presence of a Colonial District Commissioner, saying, " See what your evil *askari* did to me!"

Another place that got its name that day was *Kipriria* (place of sorrow) where the Nandi met after the murder, crying and mourning. Including the original massacre at Keet Parak, 250 men, women and children were wiped out by Meinertzhagen and his men on the 19th of October 1905.

Meinertzhagen's diary entry for that day concludes:

"So may all the King's enemies perish. The Nandi Laibon deserves some obituary notice, as he was a man of some consequence. He was both spiritual and temporal chief of all the Nandi, his office being hereditary. As both he and all his male successors were gathered today, I much regret that the dynasty must stop from today. The only people I am sorry for are his wives, for they most certainly will be buried with him as is the custom. It is their own choice to be interred dead or alive…"

It is unclear why Meinertzhagen thought he had killed Koitaleel's sons. None of them had accompanied him to Keet Parak Hill. Nor did the Nandi practice any equivalent of the Indian custom of a widow being cremated with her husband to show her devotion to him, as Meinertzhagen implied. The headless corpse of Koitaleel was interred under the Simatweet tree by which he had breathed his last and where his Mausoleum stands. None of his wives were buried with him.

Koitaleel Somoei potrait.

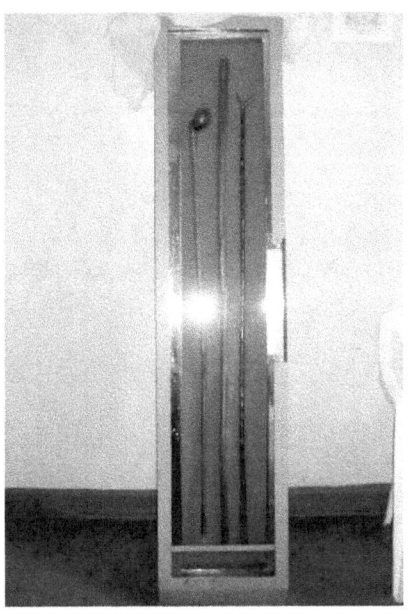

Koitaleel Somoei leadership batons brought back from Britain in 2006.

Site where Koitaleel was shot.

Koitaleel Somoei mausoleum in Nandi Hills.

Chapter 7

Grand finale

It has been said that whenever someone destroys a single life, they destroy the world entire. The saying is doubly apt of the day that Meinertzhagen murdered Koitaleel, when, in one man, the whole world of the Nandi perished. No longer the Lords of the hills and valleys, henceforth they would be as a broken spear. First, the surviving warriors would be hunted down, then the spiritual heart of the people would be torn out by the confinement of the sacred Talai clan. Finally, those left in the land would be reduced to serving as hired labourers in the lands once owned by their ancestors.

But first came the hunt, in the form of the final Nandi campaign, which was launched just two days after the assassination of the Nandi chief Oorgoiyoot. Given that the British record of the events of the 19th October understate the true number of Nandi casualties by a factor of 10, there are good grounds for scepticism towards the official figure of just 600 casualties for the final Nandi campaign. The fact that the campaign was fought against the background of a rising tide of revulsion against colonial brutality reinforces suspicion that the British would have been less than scrupulous about counting the bodies.

The Nandi recollection is that the campaign was extremely brutal and in addition to exterminating all the men of fighting age that they could find, the British also killed a multitude of innocents. There were many Nandi who fought and died bravely but, as Meinertzhagen observed, the murder of Koitaleel had left them a body without a head, unable to stand against the British onslaught.

It was during this campaign that the first rumours surfaced that Koitaleel might have been the one who was ambushed rather than the ambusher on the 19th of October. Such suspicion was eminently justified. Thus, one Colonial Office official commented sceptically of Meinertzhagen's account: "There was never such an unsuccessful ambuscade in the history of warfare. The men who are taken in the ambuscade escape without a scratch, while the 50 or more ambuscaders lose 23 killed. These facts appear to testify stronger than any evidence that treachery was not intended by the Laibon."

The cause of the fair play was taken up not only by civilian officer Walter Mayes but also by two others, Captain Cuffe and Lieutenant Wilson. The dispute led to no less than three inquiries into the incident. The testimony of Lieutenant Butler, following Meinertzhagen's lead, obscured the use of the Maxim gun. The Nandi eye witness Cheepo Rorio was not called to testify. Meinertzhagen battered his accusers with forensic cross examination and made them look like liars. Mayes withdrew from the third examination; Lieutenant Wilson offered a letter of apology. Captain Cuffe resigned in disgust rather than back down. Meinertzhagen was cleared by all three inquiries and put forward for a Victoria Cross by Butler. This recommendation was rejected, perhaps due to a feeling that, inquiry verdicts notwithstanding, something was not quite right with Meinertzhagen's story. Manning, Inspector General of the King's African Rifles, reported to the Colonial Office that "the reputation for fair dealing and honesty of the British government had been called into question."

Such concerns were not allowed to interfere with colonial plans for Nandi. The Nandi were forced into a reserve, like other indigenous peoples who had got in the way of "civilisation", leaving the remainder of their rich lands available for white settlement. To oversee this process, the British appointed a puppet Oorgoiyoot, Kibeles. The final blow to the Nandi was in 1919 when the Talai clan was banished to Kapsisiywo, an isolated island-like village in the heart of Nandi.

The Nandi had by this time already accepted their allotted place in the Empire. Still unwilling to demean themselves by serving the British as porters, they chose instead to remain true to their warrior heritage and offered their services as fighters. During the First World War, the Nandi enlisted to fight for the British in significant numbers. Around 2,000 signed up, around 20% of the adult male population of the community. Many of them were used as spies and the Nandi comprised the majority of the force that the British used to spy on German forces in Africa. As an honourable people, they should have served as reliable agents. Still, some of them betrayed the British. The cause, Brian Garfield suggests, was that in 1915, the force of spies, which included the Nandi was placed under the command of Captain Richard Meinertzhagen, the murderer of Koitaleel and the destroyer of the Nandi nation. In such circumstances, it is hardly surprising that the Nandi "betrayed" the British. In effect, they had a choice between selling out their colonial masters and betraying the memory of Koitaleel. They chose to be loyal to their dead leader even at the price of betraying their oaths of allegiance, which had been offered before the British placed them under the command of their national enemy.

Writing of his intelligence role during this war, Meinertzhagen included this spiteful anecdote about his former accuser Walter Mayes:

"In November 1914, when I was forming my Intelligence Department in the First Great War, I heard that Mayes was almost destitute, so I offered him a job, which he accepted, but within a month I had to remove him as he was embezzling Secret Service funds. He returned to his plantation and died soon afterwards."

It is certainly plausible that Mayes would have lent his credit with the Nandi to his country and helped Britain to recruit from amongst them. It is, therefore, entirely possible that he had to work with Meinertzhagen once again. However, the Nandi testify that he was far from poor, and the allegations of stealing made here have no basis beyond the word of a pathological liar.

There was a sequel to Meinertzhagen's tortured relationship with the Nandi. In 1956, Meinertzhagen returned to Kenya with the intention of seeking forgiveness from Koitaleel's family. In accordance with Nandi custom, he brought a ransom, which he intended to pay to the Oorgoiyoot's relatives. This seems remarkable in the context of Meinertzhagen's character. He was responsible for a long list of crimes, including, in the opinion of many, the murder of his wife. He did not do remorse. Yet clearly, there had been something about Koitaleel during their brief meeting that moved him to seek forgiveness from the Oorgoiyoot's family.

He did not receive it. The first person Meinertzhagen approached was Elijah Cheruiyot who was a persecutor of the Talai clan. Elijah is reported to have told him that a visit to the relatives would be difficult, as they were in exile in Kapsisiywo location 26. He also claimed it was unnecessary as the African District Council was empowered to grant forgiveness. According to a story attributed to the late Simion Mugun, a council member, Elijah introduced Meinertzhagen to the council and to the son of Kibeles, Silitia araap Beles, who pretended to be the grandson of Koitaleel. Meinertzhagen gave the money he had brought to Elijah. That some such payment was made has been confirmed by Jacob Chumba, whose father was also a member of the council. The heirs of Koitaleel never received a penny.

The account Meinertzhagen gives in his *Kenya Diary* is significantly different. To have included the incident would have been tantamount to a public confession of the murder, which he goes to such lengths to justify in that work. His account of the incident states that he was presented to the parish council at Kapsabet by the chairman Elijah. The last chief to be presented was told by Elijah, "This is the man who shot your father." Meinertzhagen asked forgiveness for "an act of war" eliciting a round of applause from the council.

In this account, Meinertzhagen manages to imply that he asked and received forgiveness from a member of Koitaleel's family, without making any admission of guilt. The murder is still justified as an act of war. Had he admitted the payment of blood money, it would have been tantamount to a public admission that he had murdered Koitaleel and that he had been lying about his crime for fifty years. Nevertheless, while he did not publicise his contrition, it is significant that this is the only incident that he describes from his 1956 visit. If the recollection recorded here is correct, Meinertzhagen's search for forgiveness would seem to provide us with the reason behind his return to the scene of his crime.

It should be remembered here that Meinertzhagen was an extremely complex character. He killed hundreds of Africans and called them savages but he also says that he was responsible for the expulsion of Christian missionaries who had been sexually abusing their converts and expresses opposition to large-scale white settlement. It is true that all his claims must be regarded with scepticism but we cannot assume that everything he said was a lie. For example, we know that even if he did not participate in Israel's war of Independence as he pretended, he was a convinced Zionist and that he was prepared to court unpopularity by his pursuit of this and other ideals. The fact that his repentance over Koitaleel's murder was marred by his unwillingness to confess his guilt in print does not mean that his request for forgiveness was mere playacting. He acted all the time in front of his peers but had no particular reason to seek the good opinion of the Nandi. His return to Kenya and his supposed payment of blood money seem to indicate that he was not, after all, a complete psychopath and that he too was subject to pangs of conscience.

Richard Meinertzhagen died in June 1967. His complex web of lies did not start to unravel until after his death and his legend was not laid to rest until the publication of Brian Garfield's, *The Meinertzhagen Mystery: the Life and Legend of a Colossal Fraud."*

As for the Nandi, the death of Koitaleel's killer could not undo the consequences of his murder. The curse that had fallen upon the people as a result of their murder of Kimnyolei was another matter, however. Kimnyolei had laid down that, when the time was ripe, the people should propitiate Assiis, by means of a sacrifice and the driving into the wilderness of an earless scapegoat. Thus, would the curse upon the Nandi be lifted.

In 1996, the leaders of the Nandi decided that the time was ripe for the breaking of the curse and the performance of the scapegoat ceremony laid down by Kimnyolei. The gathering at the site of Kimnyolei's murder included representatives from amongst his descendants and from the pororyoosiek, including those responsible for his death, the Kapsiondoi and the Kaptumoiis. After the pororyoosiek, led by the Kapsiondoi, had pleaded for forgiveness, the sacrifice was made. A cow was offered to the man standing in for Kimnyolei and a lamb to the woman representing his murdered wife. Then came the scapegoat, earless as Kimnyolei had demanded, which was driven into the forest. The spotless lamb was burnt, its smoke ascending straight to Heaven, an indication that the sacrifice was acceptable to Heaven. Ceremonial oil was then poured onto the rock in which Kimnyolei had hidden his tools of office. A week later, the rock was reportedly found split open, revealing the tools, which included those staffs that he had not passed on to Koitaleel, the *Kaaplong'enit* (a container for arrows) and the *Olomoit* or snuff box. At last, the curse of the Nandi had been broken!

Subsequent to this event, Dr Kipkoeech Araap Sambu initiated a search for items linked to Koitaleel including the "two stone-headed knobkerries," which Meinertzhagen said he had removed from the body of Koitaleel. He was assisted in this endeavour by Kibny'aanko Seroney, Joshua Chepkwony, Dr Kipkoeech Muge and Dr Joe Sang. Kibny'aanko Seroney approached Richard Meinertzhagen's son, Randle Meinertzhagen. On being asked about the knobkerries, Randle fetched instead three staffs, which turned out to be the sacred staffs of the murdered Oorgoiyoot. The staffs were similar to those that can be seen in the photos of Kibeles, the puppet that the British had appointed in place of Koitaleel. Moreover, the elders from amongst his descendants were able to identify the staffs and their roles. Randle surrendered these most willingly saying,

"Of course! Africa is where they belong!"

Though unable to put right greater wrongs that his father might have committed, Randle nevertheless, seized the opportunity to do what was within his power to lay to rest the ghosts of the past.

How these staffs came into Meinertzhagen's hands is obscure. It is theoretically possible that Koitaleel took them to the "peace conference" and that they were removed from the Oorgoiyoot's body by Meinertzhagen who, for reasons known only to himself, described them as two knobkerries. Yet the mandate of the meeting at Keet Parak did not fall under the auspices of the Royal staffs. This suggests that, at some point after the murder of Koitaleel, Meinertzhagen or an agent deputed by him ransacked Koitaleel's homestead and seized his symbols of office.

Kibny'aanko Seroney and Dr Muge took the staffs home to Kenya where they were placed in a glass case provided by Joshua Chepkwony, chairman of Kass FM. The return of the royal sceptres to Nandi attracted great crowds and was the occasion for the shedding of many joyful tears. The Nandi were joined in their rejoicing not only by their Kalenjin brothers and sisters but by every tribe and tongue in the nation of Kenya. On that day, Kenyans put aside their differences and united in praising the Nandi chief Oorgoiyoot, Koitaleel Somoei araap Kimnyolei and his unquenchable thirst for freedom.

Bibliography

Bartlett, H Moyse (1956), "*The King's African Rifles: A study in the Military history of East and Central Africa 1890-1945.*" Gale and Polden, Aldershot, UK.

Capstick, Peter Hathaway (1997), *Warrior: The Legend of Colonel Richard Meinertzhagen (1878-1967)*. St Martin's Press, New York, USA.

Churchill, Winston S (1908), *My African Journey* Hodder and Stoughton, London, U.K.

Cocker, Mark (1989), *Richard Meinertzhagen: Soldier, Scientist, Spy*. Secker and Warburg, London, UK

Garfield, Brian (2007), *The Meinertzhagen Mystery: The Life and Legend of a Colossal Fraud*. Potomac Books Inc, Washington DC, USA.

Hardy, Ronald (1965), *The Iron Snake*. Collins Clear-Type Press, London and Glasgow, U.K.

V.Harlow and E.M.Chilver (1965), *History of East Africa volume 2*. Clarendon Press, Oxford UK.

Lord, John (1970), *Duty, Honor, Empire: The Life and Times of Colonel Richard Meinertzhagen*. Random House, New York.

Matson, A.T. (1972), *Nandi Resistance to British Rule 1890-1906*. East African Publishing House, English Press, Nairobi, Kenya.

Matson, A.T. (1993), *Nandi Resistance to British Rule: The Volcano Erupts*. African Studies Centre, Cambridge UK.

Meinertzhagen, Richard (1957), *Kenya Diary 1902- 1906*. Oliver and Boyd, Kynoch Press, UK.

Miller, Charles (1971), *The Lunatic Express: An Entertainment in Imperialism*. Macdonald and co. London, UK.

Orchardson, Ian Q (1961), *The Kipsigis*. East African Literature Bureau, Nairobi, Kenya.